Single
ALL THE
WAY

KATE WATSON

For everyone who starts decorating for Christmas before (American) Thanksgiving.
You're my people.

CHAPTER ONE

JULIET

"*No.*"

My mom says this with the kind of gravity that should be reserved for mothers who've learned their daughters volunteered as tribute in the next Hunger Games and not for mothers who've learned their daughters dumped the guy they were supposed to take to their sister's wedding.

"Yes," I say into the phone.

My 2005 Nissan Sentra creaks around the corner of the packed parking garage. My apartment complex is too big for how many spaces there are. And okay, I admit that I'm kind of not supposed to park in the covered parking because I'm technically subleasing and my roommate officially gets the covered spot. But whatever. It's December in Chicago, which means it's windy, rainy, and colder than an econ professor's heart.

Plus, I hate parking on the roof. I always get stuck on the roof.

"Juliet, did you have to end things with *another* guy after only three dates right before your sister's wedding?"

"Mom." I scan the floor for an open spot. Management has strung garlands and Christmas lights around the pillars, but not even Christmas cheer can fix this conversation with my mother. "I stopped seeing Rob because we had the chemistry of baking soda and water."

"So you blended together seamlessly! That's a good thing!"

"No, we had no reaction to each other. We were bland."

My mother's groan fills my ear just as I see a car backing out of a spot in the middle of the final floor of the covered parking. Success! I speed up the ramp, ready to claim that spot, but another car whips around the corner from the opposite side of the garage. I gasp.

It's *White Prius*.

My nemesis.

He's circling the garage, too.

I fumble and drop my phone, but instead of falling onto my lap, it smacks my collarbone and then slides down my v-neck sweater, settling between my navel and the itchy wool that definitely would have benefited from an undershirt today. I grip the steering wheel and speed up like a Formula 1 racer, reaching a dangerous pace for such a tight garage.

I don't care.

This guy beats me every flipping time. How is it that we have the same schedule almost every Tuesday and Thursday ... except that he gets off a full nine seconds before me? *Every time?*

"I don't see what chemistry has to do with your sister's wedding," my mom's voice sounds from next to my belly button. "Tell him you made a mistake and just invite him to come. Please! You can dump him at the reception if you want!"

White Prius has sped up, too, and our headlights are in a staring contest. It's almost like we're playing chicken, with how close we're getting. "Rob leaned in for a kiss and I held my hand up in front of his lips and blurted, 'High five!' *High. Five.* Do you really think he'd want to come to Jocelyn's wedding after that?"

White Prius's lights are so bright, I can barely see anymore. My pulse is racing harder than that one time I threw up after winning a burpees contest in high school. I'm so close, I can practically taste it!

I floor it.

Holy cow.

I'm going to make it. That spot *will* be mine!

But then—

"NO!" I scream.

A snowy white cat darts in front of my car, and I have to slam on my brakes to keep from hitting it. My heart hammers out of my chest as I see the animal zoom in between two cars.

"What's wrong?" Mom yells. "Are you hurt? What happened?"

White Prius turns into my spot. My shoulders slump. I don't even bother circling the floor one more time. I head straight for the top level of the parking garage, where fat raindrops slap my windshield. "I almost hit a cat racing White Prius," I say flatly. "And I'm not bringing Rob."

"Juliet, you RSVP'd for *two*."

"And I'll only bring *one*. Why does it matter?"

"It matters because that spot is already gone and a wedding at The Windsor costs *five hundred dollars per plate*! It's too late to invite someone else, and you know Sandra Whitley will examine every one of our guests and lament who she could have invited, instead."

I'm about to say, "So?" when I hear a hiccup through the phone. I don't know if Mom is on the verge of tears or a breakdown.

"Please find someone," she pleads. "Or I'll set you up with one of the servers."

"You win. I'll find someone," I tell her, because she's been extra stressed lately with the wedding and because I'm only twenty-four years old and don't need my mom to set me up. "Love you."

Fluorescent lamps dot the top of the garage, reflecting off the rain slick pavement. I see an open spot near the stairwell and pull in. Then I turn off the car and lean my head on the back of the headrest, my fingers still wrapped around the peeling pleather steering wheel. As much as I try to stop myself, my fingers instantly find a place where the faux leather has separated from the rest of the material and start picking.

I let out a big sigh. "In ten seconds, you will take your hands off the steering wheel, grab your bag, pull out your umbrella, open the door, and run like h-e-double-hockey-sticks through this downpour. Okay?"

Okay.

I count down from ten, and when I reach one, I brace myself. And ... go!

Freezing rain assaults me, and I shiver instantly. I forgot my coat at the office, but as I pop my umbrella, I get shielded from the worst of it. It's so windy, the rain is coming sideways. My heels splash water as I rush for the sheltered stairwell. Just as I reach cover, I drop my umbrella to the side ...

And the wind rips it from my hand.

"No!" I dart back into the storm, rain hitting me like spitballs from an elementary schooler, but the umbrella flies through the air and sails over the far edge of the garage. I spin on my heel and run back to the stairs, panting.

Wow, Universe. Just wow.

By the time I'm downstairs and have crossed the little alley to my complex's entrance, I'm freezing and halfway soaked.

Silent Night is playing over the speakers in the lobby. I hang my head as I pass a Christmas tree surrounded by fake presents. Frigid water streams down from my honey blonde hair to the tip of my nose. Then I hear the ding of the elevator.

My head flies up. I *never* get the elevator when I come in. Several yards ahead of me, a man steps on to the elevator. His own umbrella is closed and dripping water across the terrazzo floor.

"Hold it!" I call, and I see him turn quickly and start pressing the hold button.

It doesn't do anything. "Sorry," he says, jamming the button. "It never seems to—"

But I gasp, cutting him off. It's *him*. White Prius! I've seen him play this trick before. He always gets on ahead of me and he always pretends to press the button to hold the elevator but never actually does! The jerk! He probably lives on the third floor, while I'm up on the sixteenth. "Then stick your foot out!" I snap, running. The doors start to close as my shoes strike the puddle of water left from his umbrella.

With a yelp, I skid forward, arms flailing. He sticks his foot out to catch the door. The heavy metal door knocks into his foot but doesn't stop.

I crash into him just in time to save us both from the homicidal doors.

"Whoa!" he cries as I fall on top of him. We topple backwards.

My forehead bumps into his mouth, and he hisses, even as he falls to the ground with me on top of him. We land with a wet, painful thud.

"Sorry!" I say, putting my hands on his surprisingly firm pecs. I push up enough to see him. "Are you okay?" He's so warm that I linger longer than I should getting off him.

"Fine," he grumbles, putting a hand to his generous lip. Have his lips always been that full, or did I—

Yup. I gave him a fat lip. I slide the rest of the way off of him and scramble to my feet. He props himself up onto his elbow, and his wavy black hair flops in front of his face. He has a black beard that's the perfect mix of manly and manicured and a

5

young Oscar Isaac vibe that I should love. Instead, I've hated his handsome face since the first time he let the elevator door close on me.

Although, it's not quite so loathsome now. His wide, low-lidded dark eyes smolder. Gran would call him charming. Anyone would call him sexy.

I crouch next to him, grimacing. "I really am sorry. My feet hit a slick patch and I, well, you saw what happened."

"I felt what happened, too." He arches a thick, dark eyebrow.

And he's loathsome again.

"Ugh." I stand, running a hand down the back of my hunter green corduroy skirt. Except, that's not my skirt I feel. It's my tights. My skirt is currently riding somewhere around my hips. I tug it down fast while he gets up. I really, *really* hope he didn't notice.

If he did, he's at least gentlemanly enough not to mention it. He shakes the sludge from the back of his coat, and I do my best not to marvel at how insanely long his eyelashes are. When he looks up, it's to see me gaping at him.

"What?" he asks, his eyes darting left to right. "Is there something on my face?"

I give myself a mental shake, glad I'm too cold for the heat in my cheeks to do anything but thaw me slightly. "Just, uh, noticing your fat lip."

He tuts and touches the swollen bottom lip carefully. "Is it that bad?"

Bad is not the word any woman would use to describe his lips, even if he is a jerk. "You'll want to put some ice on it when you get up to your apartment," I say.

At the mention of "up," both White Prius and I look to the floor location indicator above the elevator doors. It's still on L.

And beneath that L is ...

Mistletoe.

Who in the White Christmas put up mistletoe in an elevator?

I'm closer to the control panel, but he leans into me, and for a moment, I freeze. He's not going to kiss me, is he?

But no, he reaches past me and presses the button for the twelfth floor.

Phew.

Him pressing the button for the twelfth floor explains why I've seen him with Mrs. Kikuchi in the lobby, though. He must live next to her. She had a hip replacement right after I moved in, and I helped her on the weekends when her insurance wouldn't cover a home health nurse. We're tight now.

"What floor?" he asks, his face right next to mine.

My breath catches. "Uh, sixteen?"

"Do you not know where you live?"

He smells like a spruce tree, and his scent makes me want to deck the halls. "Huh? Oh, yes, I know where I live. Sixteen." I give him a glare so he knows I caught his sarcasm.

"Okay." He presses the button and returns to standing straight.

The elevator starts moving, and a shiver runs through me. In the excitement of crashing into White Prius, I forgot how utterly freezing I am.

"Cold outside, isn't it?" he says.

I lift my eyebrows. "Yup. Sure is."

From the corner of my eye, it looks like he winces. *Really, White Prius?* I'm almost glad for all the times he *didn't* let me get on the elevator with him. How many awkward, inane conversations did I dodge on this relic of an elevator? What should take a solid fifteen seconds with no other stops usually takes closer to thirty.

Which we're pushing as it is. What floor—

SCREEEEEK.

The elevator whines and grinds to a hard stop that makes White Prius and me stumble. The lights flicker. White Prius catches himself on the guardrail, and I catch myself on his arm.

"What the—" he says. The lights go off completely, and then a moment later, emergency lights come on, much dimmer than the usual ones.

I'm still clutching his forearm, and he's still letting me. His gaze flits back and forth between the eleven on the floor indicator and the control panel. He presses the twelve again. And again. The elevator car doesn't move.

Um.

"Should we press the emergency button?" I ask.

"Give me a second," he says. He steps up to the elevator doors and pries his fingers in between the doors, elbows up. Then he pulls. Even through his trench coat, the strain of his back muscles is evident.

And then it budges! An inch becomes two. What looks like a brick wall appears before his face, but a foot above his head, I see the next floor.

"Help me pull," he says.

"What for?" I ask, shuddering with cold. I'm still wet, and those few inches of space are letting a lot of cold air in. "The door to the floor above us is closed, and I couldn't fit through that small of a gap even if the door was fully open. Also, I'm pretty sure at least one of the *Final Destination* movies has someone trying to climb out of an elevator like this just to have it start up and cut them in half. So while this was an impressive display, and all, I'm not getting cut in half to prove that you were strong enough to save us. I'd rather let the fire department help."

I press the Emergency Call button at the same time that White Prius drops his elbows and steps away from the doors.

The doors slide back closed.

"I didn't think of that," he admits. He stretches his triceps behind his head. It must have taken a lot of strength to keep the doors open when they were fighting to shut like that.

We both stand next to each other, staring at the call box. Nothing happens.

I press the button again. We wait another ten seconds. Twenty. I'm so cold, my goosebumps have goosebumps. My teeth chatter hard together. I fold my arms, hoping to retain what little heat my body still has.

"I don't think the button is working," he says.

"I gathered that," I snap before closing my eyes with a huff. "Sorry, that was rude."

"It's more than understandable," he says in a rich voice. It's like eating homemade caramel sauce directly from the spoon.

The thought makes my stomach growl. Except, the sound is so loud, White Prius looks up and around in alarm.

"What was that?"

Should I let him think it was the elevator? I could. But my stomach is going to growl again, and it takes twenty minutes for hunger pangs to pass, which is probably the amount of time we'll be on this piece of junk elevator until the fire department gets here, and then White Prius will tell the rescue team the elevator was making all sorts of crazy sounds as we're getting out of here, but then my stomach will growl again when we're being checked for injuries, and an entire team of hot firemen will realize that my stomach is so loud that it can literally be mistaken for a broken piece of heavy machinery, and I will wish I'd been cut in half by the elevator trying to scramble up to the twelfth floor.

"That was me. I missed dinner."

He doesn't answer. Figures. Hunger pangs are probably beneath him, judging by those Italian shoes of his. I know for a fact that those things are worth more than my entire outfit, bag included. I went to Europe with my high school choir and saw shoes just like those in Milan. This guy might live in Riviera Apartments, but his wardrobe could rent the top floor of the Windsor Hotel.

A moment later, I hear a snap on his briefcase, a rustle, and then he nudges my arm. I look down to see a protein bar.

Guilt heats my cheeks, and I shake my head. He's a lot harder to hate in person than he is behind the steering wheel. Or on the other side of a closing elevator door.

"Thanks, but we'll be out of here soon enough," I say.

Besides, I have a twenty-four pack of Snickers in my bag that I'm too embarrassed to pull out.

Yes, you read that right: a twenty-four pack.

Judge away.

"I hope you're right. But I think we should probably call 911." He's already dialing when I pull my phone out to see I don't have service. Not that I ever do. To get reception in here, I think you need 9G.

Which he has. "Hi, I'm stuck in an elevator at Riviera Apartments in Pilsen." He gives the operator the address. He pauses. "Nate Cruz. Nathaniel Oscar." He pauses again. "No, someone else is with me." He angles the bottom of the phone away from his mouth. "What's your name?" he whispers.

"Juliet Shippe."

He speaks into his phone. "Her name is Juliet—" He looks at me and mouths, *middle name?*

"Louise. Juliet Louise Shippe."

"Juliet Louise Shippe," he says. "Their conversation continues, with him answering questions, pausing, and answering more. "Yes," he says. "I have Type 1 Diabetes. No, I don't need insulin. I took some in the car just a minute ago." He looks at me questioningly. I shake my head. "No, Juliet said she doesn't have any medical conditions." He pauses, then blurts, "Did you say *six hours?*"

"What?" I mouth, my teeth chattering.

His nostrils flare, and his eyes drop to my chattering teeth. His thick brows thread tightly together. "It's getting cold in here, and Juliet got drenched from the storm." He nods. "All right. Okay. And what if one of us freezes during the wait?" The olive skin above his beard flushes. His eyes flit to mine. "I'm going to need you to give her that message directly. I'll put you on speaker."

A moment later, the 911 operator is on speaker and Nate is holding his phone closer to me. "Hello, Ms. Shippe?" the woman says in a firm voice. I say hello. "Listen, it sounds like you're already cold and wet. We expect freezing weather tonight, and that elevator car won't retain much heat."

"It didn't have any to start," I say, because I'm all about the jokes.

The operator isn't. "Miss, this is serious. You're at risk of hypothermia. Do you know how to prevent hypothermia?"

Yes, I do.

"Noo …" I lie, because I don't like where this is headed.

"You need to take off your wet clothes, Mr. Cruz needs to take off his dry clothes, and you two need to get real close, real quick under whatever coat or jacket you two have."

"No," we say in unison.

"Yes," she barks. "There are power outages all over the city, and I can't guarantee anyone will be there for at least six hours, maybe longer. I'm not having a preventable death on my conscience tonight. Now strip and cuddle, pronto. And call me back if you need me."

I stare dumbly at White Prius, AKA Nathaniel Oscar Cruz.

He ends the call and stows his phone with a sigh. Then he runs a hand through his wavy black hair, and I'm momentarily captivated. Poe Dameron wishes he had Nate's hair.

"You know, she may have a point."

"Not happening."

He exhales long and slowly, and it's so long-suffering, I want to shake the patronizing right out. "Juliet, be reasonable."

"Be reasonable?" I snap. "What about my unwillingness to strip and snuggle with a stranger is unreasonable?"

"The fact that you could get hypothermia. Or did you miss that part?"

"Come on, hypothermia? That's one of those plot devices in movies that drives people to sleep together ... or go all cannibal on their friends."

Something you should know about me: I can get pretty absurd.

Nate obviously agrees with my mental self-assessment. "Which are you accusing me of? Trying to sleep with you or eat you? I assure you, I couldn't be less interested in either."

"Now you're just being rude."

A choked sound escapes his throat. He shakes his hands toward the ceiling in frustration purer than Gran's vanilla extract.

"Fine. Sit there and freeze to death. See if I care."

I cluck my tongue and fake a pout. "Aw, you don't care about me?"

He spots the mistletoe, yanks it from where it's hanging, and steps on it. Then he backs up against the side of the elevator and slides down to his butt.

I follow suit.

Looks like White Prius and I are stuck in another standoff.

Ask me who's going to win.

CHAPTER TWO

NATE

A stomach rumbles so loudly, I have to pause to consider if it's mine.

It's not. Yet, at least.

"I don't suppose you want that protein bar now, do you?" I say. The words sound bitter, as if she mortally offended me by declining my offer of food and warmth. What is wrong with me?

The woman—Juliet—is on the ground across from me. The elevator isn't large by any means. It fits maybe six people comfortably, although I've seen double that pack on before. If we both stretched our legs out, our feet would intertwine.

Not that I'm thinking of intertwining anything with the woman. Juliet, I remind myself. I've seen her a lot in the six months since she moved here. She is a pest.

An obnoxiously pretty pest.

Let me tell you all the reasons she bugs me:

First, I know for a fact that she's subleasing her apartment and that her "roommate," Lisa, has a car parked permanently in covered parking while she teaches English in Costa Rica. Mrs. Kikuchi is Riviera Apartments' resident gossip, and she gave me the full scoop when Juliet first moved in.

What that means is that every Tuesday and Thursday when I see that olive green Sentra circling the garage, Juliet is trying to steal someone's spot.

Not cool.

Second, no matter how many times the elevator closes on her face, she still thinks this will be the time where the doors will magically stay open. The elevator sucks! The call button didn't even work tonight! Does she think I'm just sitting here like some jerkwad, pretending to jam the buttons so I can have a good laugh when it closes on her face? Or does hope spring eternal in that distracting head of hers?

Maybe if she stopped circling the covered spots and went straight up to the top level of the garage like she's *supposed* to, she'd beat me to the elevator for once.

Third, she is the worst upstairs neighbor.

I live directly below her on the fifteenth floor. How do I know I live directly beneath her? The fire escape. She likes to talk to people while she's outside, even when it's freezing. She especially likes talking to her grandmother, Gran. Truth be told, the way she talks to people is endearing, but I still wish she wasn't out there at all. And then when she finishes her call, she stays out for a while. What does she stay out for? What is so fascinating that she has to disturb my peace so constantly?

Have I mentioned how loud she is? Because that's numbers four through four hundred. She makes a daycare sound like a day spa. The woman wears her heels in the apartment rather than kicking them off. Who wears shoes in their living space? Heathens, that's who. She has what I can only assume are dance parties with elephants, based on the bass that vibrates through the ceiling along with her stomping. And her bladder must be on a timer. Every morning at 3 am, I hear her get up, and a minute later, I hear the toilet flush. The second she crashes back onto her bed, I hear it like she's right on top of me.

Above me, I mean.

Why do my ears feel hot? Why is she glaring at me like I just laughed at the elevator doors closing on her face?

"You know, it looks like we're going to be stuck here for a while," she says. "Anything you'd like to say to me?"

Her knees are tucked toward her chest. Her thick stockings look dry enough, but her sweater and hair are visibly damp. I would offer her my coat, but I think she'd slap my face. It's not cold enough yet that I'm uncomfortable, but she has to be. The tip of her nose is red.

"Like what?" I ask.

"Like, I don't know, sorry for being so ungentlemanly all the time?"

Her button nose actually scrunches, and the elevator's dim emergency lights reflect from her green eyes, making them look less emerald and more hunter. Her bouncy blonde hair is normally wavy, but it's both flatter and curlier than normal, no doubt because of the freezing rain she had to walk through. She's almost impossibly cute but also just menacing enough that I would never, ever tell her that.

"Do you want my coat?" I ask, confused.

"Keep thinking." She gestures around us.

"Are you talking about the elevator? You saw that the buttons are broken." I point up at the worthless panel.

"Oh, really? Then how do the floor buttons work? I notice you have no problem getting it to go up."

I can't help it. I roll my eyes. "Did you not see my foot almost get caught in the door?" I gesture to it for effect. "You had to hurl yourself through and almost got caught, too. Or did you think I was making it up?" She narrows her eyes while I widen mine. "You did! All this time, you've thought I was fake-jabbing

15

the button, haven't you?" Color rises to her cheeks, but that glare isn't going anywhere. "You pressed the call button yourself. Nothing happened." I'm gesturing everywhere now. My foot, the panel, her, the doors, everywhere. I naturally talk with my hands, and while it can serve me in my job, it makes me feel out of control now.

Calm down, Nate. You know better than anyone how to "be seen and not heard." Channel some chill.

I take a deep, steadying breath. When I was growing up and stuck at whatever party my parents needed me as an accessory for, I would sit in the corner and skip count backward from one hundred. When two's got easy, I moved to three's. As I got older, I did it in Spanish, then in Portuguese, then finally alternating each language with each number. It occupied my mind and helped me to look like the perfect son they expected me to be.

I don't need to skip count backwards to get a hold of myself, fortunately. The breathing helps. "The buttons are broken. Including the floor buttons, on occasion."

She cocks her head to the side, but the accusation in her eyes shifts to suspicion. "Yet my button works every time."

"Mine doesn't," I say. "I usually walk the last few floors after I stop at—" I cut myself off. My detour is none of her business. And that makes it pique her interest.

"Yes?"

"Nothing."

She eyes me. A gust of cold air passes through the ceiling vent, and she shudders but doesn't stop. "Secret lover?"

I snort. "No."

"Someone you owe money to?"

"Not even close."

"Friend?"

"In a manner of speaking."

"Then why wouldn't you just say that?"

I exhale all the chill I managed to channel. "Because you and I don't know each other, and it doesn't concern you."

She shakes her head. "Oh, so it's going to be like that, is it? You get to be a jerk to me constantly, and now we're stuck here for half the night, and rather than talk, you're going to freeze me out?"

"Freeze you—" I feel my nostrils flare. "That's funny coming from the woman I'm trying to keep alive."

Her jaw drops. "You're only trying to help me because you feel guilty!"

"What should I feel guilty for?"

"Because you took the spot I was gunning for—AGAIN."

I sit up. "A spot you're not allowed to have! Your roommate already claimed the covered spot allotted to your apartment, and the lease dictates that only one car per apartment gets a covered spot. Any other vehicles are required to use the additional parking on the top floor of the garage."

Her cheeks are rose red now. She looks like she's about to fight me, but instead, a small sound escapes her lips. "Oh."

Shoot. "Did you not know?" I feel bad thinking of the months on end that she's been cursing me out for taking a covered spot. If she really didn't know, no wonder she thinks I'm such a jerk.

She bites the inside of her cheek, making her lips into even more of a cupid's bow. Her voice gets higher, and she phrases her admissions like questions. "Um. Yeah, I kind of did. I didn't think anyone would know about my roommate." My chest tightens with annoyance. How can she be so appealing while admitting to breaking rules? And why does she look suspicious again? "Hey, how did you know, anyway?"

"Are you serious? How am I the bad guy in this scenario?"

She tugs her eyebrows down. She's probably five-two without her heels, but she has a "Though she be but little, she is fierce" vibe that Shakespeare would approve of. "I'm not saying

17

you're the bad guy, but I'm a twenty-four year-old woman living by myself in Chicago, and now I find out that a man in my complex knows more about me than I know about him. Believe me, it's natural for me to be wary. So I repeat: how did you know about my roommate?"

I sigh, leaning my head back on the elevator wall. I'm almost as bummed to find out she's only twenty-four as I am reluctant to tell her about my detour. But she has a point. "I guess I'll tell you about my friend after all."

CHAPTER THREE

JULIET

Over the last twenty minutes, I've learned a lot about Nathaniel—sorry, Nate—Cruz:

First, he is a stickler for the law. Like, there's no way this guy has ever spit out a piece of gum while walking, even if it's already passed the "almost out of flavor" stage and reached full "this is the grossest thing I've ever tasted; how can I live with this gum in my mouth for another second?" level. The law is his best friend.

Second, but related: he hates injustice. While he has no problem letting me get soaked in freezing rain on the top floor of the parking garage in a Chicago winter, he takes real issue with the rights of landlords compared to tenants, as evidenced by the fact that he took Mrs. Kikuchi on pro bono as a client when she ran into a snag with her lease following her husband's death last year. It turns out Nate's "friend" that he was so cagey about is Mrs. Kikuchi.

Third, he really, really does not want me to die of hypothermia.

"You need to take that sweater off, and we need to huddle to get you warm."

"I'm fine." I shiver audibly.

"Take my coat."

"Then *you'll* be cold."

"I'm not wet."

"I'll be fine." But then an icy shudder overtakes me, and Nate jumps up.

"That's it. I'm fixing this now."

I've never had a guy go alpha on me before, and I've always kind of hated it in movies, but I am not mad about it.

Not at all.

He stands, and I brace myself for what's next. But instead of pulling me up and making me see reason—which I genuinely realize I'm *not* doing; I blame the cold—he pulls out his phone and makes a call.

It's to Mrs. Kikuchi. He explains that we're stuck, asks her to bring as many blankets and warm clothes as she can, and then he sits beside me under his coat and wraps his arms around me.

I don't protest for a second. But I'm also a bit too cold to talk.

A few minutes later, there's a knock on the elevator doors above us.

Nate uses his insane back and arm muscles to pry the doors open again, and Mrs. Kikuchi drops down blankets and clothes to us.

"Hello, dear!" she says like we've just run into each other in the hallway. "I see you two have finally met, then," she says significantly.

Oh.

I've gotten to know Mrs. Kikuchi pretty well in the last six months. Helping her with her recovery led to weekly visits where I drop off *kolaches* from the Czech deli down the street and she shares all the hot gossip. A couple of months ago, she told me she wanted to set me up with a "young friend" from the complex who was "absolutely dreamy." She talks about him every week.

Mrs. Kikuchi has been talking about Nate.

"Thanks, Mrs. K!" I say as Nate grunts.

"Don't have *too* much fun in there," she says.

Nate grunts again, and when I've taken the last of her care package, his arms shake and he lets go.

We both step back as the doors slam.

"Stay safe!" she yells through the doors.

"We will," he calls back. "Thanks again!"

Well, that's adorable.

He breathes heavily, shaking out his arms and rolling his shoulders.

"Could you turn around while I get changed?" I ask, shivering.

"Of course," he says. He faces the corner where the buttons are, and I turn my back to him and peel my wool sweater off quickly. I throw on a waffle knit shirt and then a knit sweater that looks like it came from the Grandmother section at Walmart. Then I layer another sweatshirt over it, a gray one featuring a calico kitten sitting in a stocking. And the kitten is wearing a Santa hat. And beneath the kitten, it reads in a festive script, "The stockings were hung by the chimney with cats."

I am never giving this sweatshirt back.

With the wettest of my clothes off, I remove my damp skirt and put a pair of sweats over my dry stockings. Then I slip on three pairs of socks. I feel so much better, it makes me wonder if I was in more danger than I thought. My head feels clearer, too, clear enough to realize how stupid I was to fight him about removing my sweater and putting on his coat.

I'm a button pusher. I know this about myself, but that was next level.

Nate is still facing the wall, stretching out his sore arms.

"How's it coming?" Nate asks.

The metal is just shiny enough that I can see his reflection. His eyes are squeezed shut.

Okay, that's *insanely* adorable.

"Did you see something in the reflection?" I ask suspiciously.

"No! What do you think I am, some thirteen year-old perv from an 80s movie?"

I grin. This guy is easier to wind up than a watch.

"I'm teasing. I can see you *squeezing* your eyes shut. You're precious."

"Precious? No. I'm a grown man."

"How old are you, Grown Man?"

"Thirty-one."

Dang it. I was kind of hoping he was more like twenty-nine. It feels less creepy for me to find him hot if our ages are both in the same decade.

"Why didn't you want to tell me about Mrs. Kikuchi?"

"Are you still getting dressed?"

"I'm the one asking the questions."

He bumps his head against the metal one, two, three times.

"Okay, fine, I'm done," I say. "You can turn around."

I sit on the ground, arms slung around my knees. He turns, gives me a once over, and looks at my clothes tossed haphazardly on the ground.

He scoops up my wet things, folds them, and puts them in the opposite corner from us.

Then he sits against the wall next to me and puts Mrs. Kikuchi's three blankets over us.

"Getting a little familiar, aren't you?"

He drops his gaze to me. "You're messing with me, aren't you?"

"Oh, yes. Constantly. You're just so *easy*. Your siblings must have a field day with you."

"I'm an only child."

"You think?"

He shakes his head. "How many siblings do you have?"

"I meant it about me asking the questions. Why wouldn't you tell me about Mrs. Kikuchi?"

Nate rests his head against the wall behind us. "I try to be a good person. If you advertise that you help people in need, you're not actually a good person."

"Fair point. You two seem close, though. Like closer than a lawyer and his client."

"I stop by most nights and watch Jeopardy with her."

"You don't get home from work until seven or eight at night."

"She records it for me."

Could these two be more darling?

"Sometimes we play cards," he continues. "Sometimes I bring her dinner, other times she gives me a *kolache* from that Czech deli down the street because she knows how much I like them."

"Wait, those *kolaches* are for you? *I'm* the one who gives her those!"

"What?"

"Yes, I bring them to her every Friday when I stop by after class. We chat for a bit. She always told me she loves them!"

"She does," he assures me. "She has the appetite of a bird. I think she feels like she needs to pay me back for helping her with the rent situation."

"Have me pay you back is more like it," I mutter.

He's been the salt to my vinegar this whole time, but now that he knows I've been teasing him, he seems to loosen up. "Yeah, I guess so. Mrs. K is sly. You know, she's always telling me about this 'young friend of hers' who visits her on Fridays. I didn't realize that was you."

I laugh. "Funny. She's been talking to me about her 'dreamy young friend with a heart of gold,' too. Looks like she's trying to set us up."

I don't tell Nate that she was right, though. He may be as annoying as my twin sister rummaging through my closet, but he is absolutely dreamy.

He's also thirty-one and probably graduated from law school when I graduated from high school.

So does it matter that he's single, goes out of his way to help an elderly woman, and has the sexiest kind of hair and beard a man can have? He's the perfect blend of manly and kempt.

In a word: hot.

Also, as much as I accused him otherwise, he *is* a gentleman. He wanted to help me tonight, even when he thought I was a brat who steals parking spots. I believe him about the elevator, too. The call button obviously didn't work, and the elevator doors really did almost cut us in half.

Suffice it to say, I'm no longer angry at Nate Cruz.

Now if I could stop myself from getting a crush on him.

Maybe that sounds alarming, but it isn't. I fall in and out of like with someone every few weeks. The crush is inevitable. The commitment, on the other hand, is very much not. I've never maintained chemistry with anyone—*anyone*—past the third or fourth date. It's a big joke to my family, especially because my twin sister is getting married to a guy I went out with. In fact, he didn't even get a third date.

At least, not with me.

We joke that he's my ex, but that's dramatically overstating it. After the second date, I knew I wasn't interested, but Jocelyn was, so she just ... took my place.

Are you grimacing thinking about it? I'm grimacing remembering it. Especially considering that her fiancé didn't find out about our switcheroo for two more dates. Zach thought he'd simply gotten her name wrong. He thought she'd "finally mellowed" after he "got to know the real Jocelyn."

Because that's not hurtful at all.

I'm the firework of the family while Jocelyn is a never-ending candle, a steady flame that won't blow out. Tomorrow night, she's marrying into one of Chicago's premiere families, and I'm stuck in an elevator with a hot lawyer who looks at me like I'm a hyperactive Yorkie in need of a snuggle.

The snuggle part might be wishful thinking, come to think of it. But in my defense, even with the warm clothes and blankets, my hair is freezing me. My teeth chatter.

"Are you okay?" Nate asks.

"It's just my hair," I say.

He tuts and escapes from under the blankets for a moment to grab his satchel. Then he pulls out a black beanie and kneels in front of me. "I'm sorry I didn't think about this sooner."

Nate tugs the beanie over my head, his thumbs grazing my cheeks. His hands are warmer than I expected, which makes me wonder if he got under the blankets to warm me up or to get close.

I'm not mad either way. He's not the villain I painted him out to be.

Also, have you seen his cheekbones? Hello, bone structure.

"Is that better?" he studies my eyes.

"Yeah," I say. "You're warm."

"I am for now," he says. "But that'll change soon enough if I don't get under the blankets."

So it really is about the warmth, then. Bummer.

"And here I thought this was all an elaborate ploy for you to get me alone and trapped in an elevator with you," I say as he settles in beside me.

"Ha," he says. "And why would I do that?"

"Duh," I say. "Cannibal much?"

His lips quirk upward. "911 already knows we're together. If

I'm smart enough to have planned a power outage, you'd think I wouldn't have made such a careless mistake."

"That's assuming you actually called 911." I'm teasing, but he shifts under the blankets and pulls out his phone. He shows me the call, including how long it lasted. "And it's assuming you gave them your real name."

He takes out his wallet and shows me his ID. "You can take a picture of it and me, if you want. Send it to a friend. You don't have service now, but it'll go through when you have it again. Heck, you can even use my phone if you're worried."

"That's okay."

"No, do it. You're smart to be wary. Not of me, to be clear," he adds hastily. He takes a picture of his ID and attaches it to a blank text. "Here, type in your number. I don't want you to have to worry all night."

I stopped worrying as soon as he told me about Mrs. Kikuchi, but I appreciate his concern. I've put him through the ringer already, and every gesture shows me how trustworthy he really is. But I take his phone and start typing my number and my roommate's anyway.

I'm not sure why I do it. Maybe it's the fact that by this time tomorrow, Nate will be a memory, and I already want a memento from this crazy time together.

I hit send and hand him back his phone.

Nate puts it away and huddles close. The entire right side of my body is pressed against the left side of his. Warmth fills me everywhere our bodies touch.

"Thanks for the help tonight, Nate. I misjudged you."

"My pleasure," he says. "I don't mean *pleasure*," he adds.

"It's okay. I'm past worrying about you being a creep. Now I just think you're a weirdo."

Because our bodies are basically attached, when he snorts, my body moves with his. "Weirdo? Seriously?"

"The effort not to talk with your hands is overpowering your whole body."

He drops his face to look at mine. I look up and over, and I almost lose my breath.

He just keeps getting more alluring. I thought his eyes were a solid brown, but now I see bursts of amber around his pupils. His full lips spread into a small smile. "You're paying a lot of attention to my body."

Yes. Yes, I am.

"If you're going to go to all this effort to trap us together on an elevator for a cuddle session," I find myself saying, "the least I can do is pay attention."

He smiles fully, and I swoon a little.

Or a lot.

"I thought you thought I was a cannibal."

"Nah. You look like you keep close track of your macros. I'd throw your count off." I jab my elbow into him, but it lacks force. Or maybe it just stops against his rock hard side. The numbness that had overtaken my body is thawing, and with that has come an awareness of how very firm he is. "So, uh, do you come here often?"

A laugh explodes from him. "It takes a weirdo to know a weirdo, huh?"

I shrug, but inside, I squeal, because he's funny, and he clearly thinks I'm funny. I've dumped guys for not being funny before. And I've dumped them for not laughing at my jokes before, too. Nate and I are clearly never going to date, but if we're stuck together for another five hours, I plan to enjoy every second.

CHAPTER FOUR

NATE

My y stomach growls in the middle of a heated argument over which TV show is better: *The Office* or *Parks and Recreation*. Juliet is firmly Team Leslie Knope, and I'm firmly Team Jim Halpert.

Tendrils of her long blonde hair pop out from the beanie, giving her a snow bunny look that any guy would fall for. Plus, seeing her in that big goofy cat sweatshirt is more appealing than I care to admit. I've dated girls who wouldn't even let me see them without makeup. Juliet may have mascara on, but nothing about the rest of her image is carefully curated. I dig it.

And that's the last thing I need.

I date often enough. My last girlfriend and I were together for a year. We parted on friendly terms after I went out of town for a week and neither of us missed the other.

I think anyone would miss Juliet.

"It doesn't matter if you're Team Jim," she says. "Michael Scott is the main character, and because he's inferior to Leslie

Knope in every way, *Parks and Rec* is the better show based on protagonists alone."

"Michael left the show and it continued," I argue. "He literally can't be the main character."

"His absence was a character of its own," she says. "Besides, Jim isn't the main character, he's the audience's surrogate. He tells us how we're supposed to respond to the madness of the office all around him."

That's an excellent point, but it only strengthens my argument. "Exactly. And because of that, he's the protagonist. He's the one we're rooting for because he's the one we relate to."

She taps a fingernail against her teeth. "But only because we see ourselves in him. That makes *the viewer* the main character."

"Only if you're secretly in love with Pam. He has his own motivations separate from ours. Hence, he's the main character."

I don't care as much about this debate as it may appear. I just love debating. I don't do it with most people, because most people hate it.

Juliet doesn't hate it. If anything, I think she's having as much fun as I am.

"Okay, I'll give you that one," she says. "But *Parks and Rec* is still the better show. The entire cast of characters is likable and basically good, whereas *The Office's* characters are base and petty."

"Base?" I'm about to say more when my stomach growls again. Last time, it got swallowed up by our debate, but this time, it sounds like I opened my mouth to let out a roar.

"Okay, okay," she teases. "If you feel that strongly about it, I'll let you pretend *The Office* is better."

I smirk and pull my bag closer with my foot. The leather drags across the plywood floor. I hope it doesn't catch on something. "I know I've offered already, but I have a protein bar in my bag. Care to split it with me?"

29

"Can I admit something?"

"I think we're past having to ask that. Yes."

She nudges me, and I like it more than I should, considering she's twenty-four and only pressed against me because she's in duress. "I have some candy bars in my bag."

"Some? As in more than one?"

She tucks her face against my shoulder. "Just a handful."

"We've upgraded to a handful? How many do you have?"

She mumbles against my arm. "Twenty-four."

"TWENTY-FOUR! Are you okay?"

She laughs. "What?"

"Are you okay? Is that why you looked so upset in the car? Were you planning your last meal?"

She full on giggles, and the sound makes my stomach flip. "I was upset that my mom was trying to set me up for my sister's wedding because I stopped seeing the guy she thought I was taking. Why on earth would a bunch of candy bars signal my imminent demise?"

Imminent demise? The flipping in my stomach has become a whole floor routine as she drops LSAT vocab like that. She cannot know how attractive I find a command of language. Any language. "Because the effect on your insulin alone would wreak havoc on your entire body. If two dozen chocolate bars aren't a sign that you're dying, they're the cause that will put you there."

Her body shakes. I'm warm where our bodies connect, and that warmth spreads out to my extremities. "Did you think I was going to eat all of them right now? You did! Nate Cruz, give me a little credit. I may have forgotten my coat at the office and the hawk out there may have snatched my umbrella—"

"A hawk?" I repeat. "An actual hawk grabbed your umbrella?"

"No." She snorts. "It's the nickname Chicagoans have for the freezing wind that blows off of Lake Michigan." As if on cue, a frigid gust reaches us through the vent. Juliet leans in closer to me, and I want to thank the hawk. "You're not from Chicago, are you? I can't place your accent."

"I grew up splitting my time between Europe and the States." I say. "Why do they call it the hawk?"

"Because hawks are as fast as the wind and their talons as sharp as the cold that bites into you."

"Wow. That's poetic."

"Is now too soon to admit that I made that up? I actually have no clue," she says. I chuckle to myself. "Tell me about growing up internationally. That must have been cool."

She has freckles. I've never thought much about freckles before, but she has a smattering across her nose and cheeks. Her impossible cuteness must weaken my defenses, because I find myself telling her the truth, the whole truth, and nothing but the truth.

"It was good and hard. My mom is Portuguese and my dad is Spanish. They met at Northwestern and fell in love right away. When I was born, my parents lucked into some huge business decisions that paid off, and that allowed them to split their time between Europe and the States. It was cool. I had experiences most people dream of. But it also made me feel like I didn't belong anywhere."

She nods. "That *sounds* hard. Even if I'm jealous that you've probably visited the Joanine Library or spent time in the Azores or the Alhambra."

I've been to all of them multiple times. "You know your geography," I say, genuinely impressed. Most Americans don't know Spain or Portugal as well as they know France, Italy, or the UK. With every word out of her mouth, I'm more entranced by Juliet.

"I've changed majors five times."

Or not.

Alarm bells go off in my head, warning me to slow down,

watch out. Because she said she *has* changed majors. Present perfect. Meaning she's still in school.

Sometime in the last hour, my view of Juliet switched from *never ever* to *very interested*. Subconsciously, the age gap didn't feel quite so insurmountable when I thought she was working full time, when she was talking about leaving her coat at the office.

Now I'm struck with the reminder that Juliet isn't just seven years younger than I am, she's in a totally different life stage.

She looks at me expectantly. We've had so much back and forth that she must be wondering why I haven't responded to her having nearly a half dozen majors. But how do I respond? Playfully? With the disappointment that older adults always use on college kids? I feel like a dinosaur compared to her.

Be real, I tell myself.

The reality is that I'm wildly curious. I majored in psychology because analyzing people and their choices fascinates me, and transitioning to law was a natural outgrowth of it. Asking Juliet anything is as natural as breathing.

I shouldn't be as curious as I am about her, though.

You're overthinking this, a voice that sounds like my mother's says in my head.

I overthink everything. I overdo everything. I've heard that my whole life.

It's true, too. Juliet and I could be stuck in here for hours still. I can't analyze every word she says or every emotion I feel. Besides, my hunger is probably playing games with my head. I pull out my protein bar, with its macros as precise as Juliet suggested. "I need to eat something. Just a second."

She sits more upright, breaking contact with me. "Oh shoot, that's right: you have Type 1 diabetes. Are you okay? Do you need me to do anything? You don't need sugar, right?"

"No, I definitely do *not* need sugar."

"Not sure I needed the attitude with that answer, but okay."

"I'm not trying to give you attitude. But eating sugar could kill me if I don't have my insulin. And seeing as I'm stuck on an elevator for the next several hours and don't have my insulin, please don't feed me sugar if I pass out."

I expect her to feel the weight of my words and do an about face. Instead, she looks at me like I'm being ridiculous. "Do you think I'd shove a Snickers in your mouth the second you went unconscious? You'd choke before the diabetic coma could kill you. I may be young, but I'm not *that* dumb." She holds a finger up between us, making me think I'm not the only one who talks with my hands. "Also, you have a life-threatening condition that requires you to have medicine on hand at all times, but you didn't carry it with you from the car to your apartment? Why?"

My palms go sweaty. "I, uh, forgot it," I admit.

"Huh," she says. Pointedly.

"All right, I get it," I grumble.

"Excuse me?" She cocks her head so her ear is only inches from my mouth.

"I get it. I spoke sharply and made you feel dumb, but I'm the real dummy. It was a jerk move. I'm sorry."

She beams, her round cheeks like cute little balls. "You're forgiven. Besides, I was actually in nursing school for a couple of years and kind of already knew about the sugar thing and was just messing with you to see how you'd respond."

I close my eyes while I chew. "Are you crazy? Why would you do that?"

"Do what? Give up on nursing weeks before I was scheduled to take my licensing exam or ask a fake question to see how you'd react?"

I blink. "Both."

She takes a few moments to answer. "My grandma had a stroke over Christmas break a few years ago and I missed the signs. I thought she was having a migraine, and she's never fully

33

recovered because of my mistake. I couldn't do that to someone else's family."

I swallow a bite of my bar. "That's a lot of pressure to put on yourself. Don't doctors miss that kind of thing, too?"

"It doesn't matter what someone else does. It matters what *I* do. Or don't do." She pulls the blankets more closely around herself.

"What about the fake question?"

She gives me an apologetic nose scrunch. "I tend to play dumb a lot."

"You play dumb? Why would you pretend to not know something?"

"I don't know. It's probably a defense mechanism."

"What are you defending yourself against?"

"Comparisons, maybe?"

I study her. "Go on." She hems, so I press. "What else are we going to do for the next few hours?"

She sticks her bottom lip out and blows air straight up her face. "My twin sister is good at everything. She knew what she wanted from the womb, and I still don't. She already has a master's, a real job, and is getting married. I'm on my fifth major in seven years and was let go from my *unpaid* marketing internship when the firm relocated to South Carolina. Now I work ten hours a week for a non-profit and make peanuts. I'm always dating someone new. My parents would never say it outright, but they think I'm a joke."

I bristle. "So your sister has her master's and you're still in college. You're working on your degree. You have a job. You have your own place. What's not to be proud of?" I ask this as if I'm not battling my own reactions to her confession. But to hear that her family judges her makes me defensive on her behalf.

"It's not just the college thing, it's everything in my life. My family has *always* compared us. Jocelyn is the easy twin. I'm the hard one. They're not wrong. Things always work out for my sister. She works her butt off. She's dedicated and focused. When she sets her mind to something, she makes it happen. She never, ever fights back if something doesn't make sense."

"And you?"

"I set my mind to something and do well … until I don't. Or I'll hit a point with a subject where everything stalls and I see something else that's more exciting. First it was nursing, then English, chemistry, marketing, and now economics. I can't explain it. Nothing can carry my interest, because nothing ever feels right for long. And I'm just so curious all the time! I don't want to know the rule, I want to know *why* there's a rule. And no, I don't have ADHD. Believe me, I've been tested."

I put the pieces of our interaction together quickly. "Have you considered that you're gifted?"

"Ha! My sister's the genius. Not me."

"No, gifted isn't solely about IQ. It's about a different way of seeing things." I shift, but it makes us break contact, so I keep shifting until we're pressed close again. I like that we're touching, but I can't look at her as easily. I have to crane my head to see the silky smooth skin of her cheeks and neck.

Focus.

I pull my thoughts together. "You're a perfectionist, aren't you?"

"I'm a chronic underachiever, Nate."

"I'm not asking you what you achieve, but how you feel when you're *trying* to achieve something. I bet little mistakes drive you crazy."

"They drive everyone crazy."

"Ah ha. I knew it. I bet you were at the top of each of your programs when you dropped out."

"I did okay."

"Another yes. And after the parking garage and elevator and your deeply held resentment toward me, I already know you have a strong sense of justice, even if it's misguided."

"That's called revenge."

"It sounds like your family thinks you lack focus and are hyperactive—"

"To put it mildly."

"And you're obviously a quick problem solver. You knew opening the elevator door would do nothing for us while I was still pulling it open."

"True."

"Are you good at strategy games?"

"I love sudoku. And my family refuses to play *Clue* with me."

I smile. "You're gifted. Are you and your high IQ sister identical twins?"

"Ask the guy she's marrying next week how long it took for him to realize we switched places."

"Uh." I close my mouth and open it again. "I'm going to need that story later. For now, you should know that in this psych major's well-informed opinion, you are absolutely gifted."

"Ooh, do you think I'd like psychology? JK. I already dropped that one."

"Juliet."

"Just kidding," she says with that same round-cheeked smile. Her skin is like glass, and when she moves, I can smell hints of orange and mint from her damp hair. "But I don't think being a psych major qualifies you to make that judgment."

"Does interning for a year in a school's gifted and talented program qualify me?"

Her eyebrows rise. "Only if you were giving me the actual test."

"Please. Like I don't have that test memorized." I crack my knuckles for effect, but because it's under blankets, there *is* no effect. I just make a weird movement that shifts the coat off us, blasting us with the cold elevator air.

"NATE!"

"Sorry!" I adjust the blanket around us as she shivers. I put my arm around her beneath the blankets and rub her shoulder. "Half the questions were things you'd need visuals for, but I know the other half. Are you ready to do this?"

She leans her head against my shoulder. I want it to be for affection, but the feel of her cold cheek tells me it's a necessity. And I'll take it.

"I'm ready."

CHAPTER FIVE

JULIET

*N*ate is convinced that I'm gifted, whatever that means, and I'm convinced that if it gets any colder in this icebox, we're both going to pull a Walt Disney and get cryogenically frozen.

(I'm kidding. I don't actually think Walt was cryogenically frozen.)

(Or do I?)

While I'm not convinced we'll freeze, I am convinced he dislikes his job. He talked with so much more passion about that job with kids than he has telling me about his work doing corporate law at a firm called KKM.

"I think you missed your calling," I tell him.

"No, psych wasn't for me."

"But you loved working with those kids."

"All I did was administer a slapdash G&T test. You have no basis to assess my feelings about the job."

I love how much Nate loves to argue, because I do, too.

Whenever a topic comes up, I like to take the other side, just to see what happens. Does the person I'm talking to feel as strongly as they think they do? Are they as informed as they think they are? Do they know what biases led them to believe what they believe? Can they respect a different opinion, even if they disagree? I'm not trying to be annoying, but I know most people think I am. They think I'm argumentative and love to pick fights.

Nate informs me that's another trait of giftedness.

Eye roll.

"When you're a hammer, everything is a nail," I say. "You look for giftedness everywhere because working with those kids left a mark on you. You miss the job."

"I liked working with the kids," he concedes. "But I wasn't passionate about the work. Or the paycheck."

I feign shock. "You got a paycheck in your internship?"

"About that: why were you unpaid?"

"Because the Jane & Co. women were *bosses*. They made me want to figure my junk out. And they shouldn't have had to suffer through cruddy interns just because they were a startup. And they made it big."

"Do I know any of their campaigns?"

"McLadyPants is my favorite, but Sugar Maple Farms is the one that launched them. They sent me a huge bonus over the summer, actually. The CEO said it was her way of saying thanks."

Nate nods, like he recognizes both campaigns. "So you took an unpaid internship because you didn't feel like a struggling company should miss out on a quality intern." He grins like a wolf. "Innate sense of justice. Gifted."

I've fought it for the last hour, but now I laugh. "Okay, okay. You make a compelling case. But you have to admit that I do, too. You may love the law, but you're way more passionate about helping people than helping companies. Admit it."

He looks at the wall opposite us, as if staring back into his past. "Yeah, I guess you're right."

"Ha! I knew it!" I exclaim, bumping his side with my elbow a few times in victory. "So why'd you pick corporate law instead of something more meaningful?"

"I like the idea of working for a non-profit, but there's not as much money in that."

"So? Is it all about money?"

"No, but I grew up with some … privilege."

"Not just *some* privilege, Mr. International. You're crazy rich. Admit it."

"Okay, fine. We're crazy rich, but I refuse to take my parents' money."

"Why? Are they bad people?"

"No, nothing like that," he says. "My childhood was complicated. I traveled everywhere with them, complete with tutors to make sure my education didn't slip. There were so many parties and dinners, launches and ribbon ceremonies. I felt more like a prop than their kid half the time. When it came time for me to finally make my own decisions, I knew I couldn't take their advice or their money if I wanted to become my own man."

"Do you guys still talk?"

"Yes, occasionally."

"You don't have moral objections to your parents' money, only personal ones."

He nods. "Doing non-profit work or taking pro bono clients would be nice, but I'm not a good enough person to starve for my passion *or* my pride."

I pepper him with questions about his family. His parents are international real estate moguls with multiple different estates. Not homes. *Estates.*

"They'll be in Chicago for their anniversary party next weekend and will stay through Christmas."

"Are you going to go?"

"They're my parents," he says.

Nothing about Nate's parents feels catty or mean. They sound oblivious and ultra-driven. I get the sense Nate has an inferiority complex or a chip on his shoulder. A thirst to prove himself or achieve something.

But I haven't majored in psychology, so what do I know?

"Do you think they miss you or do they just want to show off their hot, successful son?"

"Hot?" He smiles that delicious, wolfish smile. "That's not how they'd talk about me, but I don't mind if you do."

I reach a hand up and squeeze his cheeks like a grandmother. His beard is softer than I expected, and it's everything I can do to not run my fingernails over it. "You know you're gorgeous."

"I know you're hungry, too," he says after my stomach roars. "Ready to bust out that Snickers?"

I yawn. "If I pass out, you can put a Snickers in my mouth if you need to. I trust you."

Nate laughs. "I'm not going to put a Snickers in your mouth."

"You know what I mean. Thanks for taking care of me, Nate."

"The night isn't over yet," he says. "I have questions about you quitting nursing right before getting licensed."

Nate pulls my bag over to us and unwraps a candy bar for me. I eat it quickly while he opens up a bottle of water and takes a sip.

"Ah," I say, content. "I am an open book, Nate Cruz. Ask away."

"Okay, Juliet Shippe, why did you feel like quitting would save more lives than simply learning more would?"

"Ouch. Do you always cut to the core?"

"I think we both know the answer to that is yes."

"I really like that about you," I admit.

"I really like that you like that about me," he says. "Now spill."

I do. And I ask him questions, and he spills. And we talk for

41

hours and hours. Every conversation is deeper and more enjoyable than the last.

Until I fall asleep.

When I rouse a bit later, it's to find that Nate's head is against mine, and he's breathing deeply. The movement is so peaceful, it sends a pleasurable wave of tingles over my body. With his neck so close, I catch the subtle, intoxicating scent of sandalwood and cedar that I somehow missed earlier when we were talking.

I'm tired, my face is cold, and I'm borderline addicted to Nate's smell, but I have enough of my wits about me to know that this is the sexiest thing that's ever happened to me.

A smoking hot European man is using his own body as my personal heating pad, pillow, and blanket.

I'm not mad about it.

Not at all.

But I'm already getting sad. I've shared more with Nate tonight than any guy I've ever dated. I've admitted things I've never told my own family. We've talked about a lot of nonsense, sure, but we've also cut through the crap in a way I've never done with anyone. There's no place for pretense when survival is on the line.

And that makes me sad for another reason.

If it takes mortal peril for me to reach emotional intimacy, how will I ever get this deep with a guy again?

Two months from now, when my crush has faded, will he look at this time as fondly as I will? I'm already nostalgic for this time together, and we're still in it. The way he cradles me into his body, even while he's asleep, puts a lump in my throat.

I want to stay awake, because I suspect that never in my life will I have a moment as glorious as this one. Being in Nate's arms makes me feel safe and, as dumb as this sounds, accepted. We've talked for hours, and he's seen behind a curtain I don't like even acknowledging. Yet here he is embracing me. It feels like this is a metaphor for something.

Or maybe my feelings have taken on a life of their own.

Either way, I plan to revel in this feeling every minute we have left.

CHAPTER SIX

NATE

a loud whirring and a flickering of lights wake me. Juliet's face is buried in my neck, and I can feel the warmth of her lips on my skin. She's okay. We're both okay.

I breathe a sigh of relief and rest my head against hers when the significance of the noise and the lights hit me.

The power is back on.

The floor indicator is flashing. It should return to the lobby automatically, but this elevator is trash. It's no surprise that the thing is waiting for instructions. That means that for the elevator to start moving, *I'll* need to move. I need to wake Juliet.

Our night has come to an end.

A wave of disappointment hits me. We talked for hours and hours, but it wasn't long enough. Falling asleep feels like squandering our time together. This night has meant something to me. I'm not ready to say goodbye.

I've always struggled to open up to the women I've dated,

not because there was anything wrong with them, but because we didn't connect emotionally.

I had no such problem with Juliet.

She teased and taunted me, but in doing so, she put us on even footing. My background, age, and upbringing didn't intimidate her. My occasionally overbearing personality didn't faze her. If anything, she challenged me more because of it. She didn't try to take me down a notch, but she didn't let me get away with anything, either.

Hour after hour, we connected. We bonded.

And now I've fallen for her.

She's twenty-four and you were a heat source to her. Don't overdramatize this, I tell myself. I blink a few times, taking in the elevator. I must have some gunk in my eye, because everything seems blurry. A loud grinding sound starts, and a moment later, warm air blows down on us.

"About time." I laugh to myself.

"Hmm? Time?" Juliet asks, sounding groggy.

"The power's back on. We're saved."

"My hero," she says simply. And then, the best thing happens: She doesn't move.

She just stays there, tucked under my arm, her legs bent over mine, her head cradled against me. Could she be as reluctant as I am to end the night? How long can we reasonably stay like this?

My stomach answers that question for me with a grumble that makes Juliet giggle. "Want that candy bar now?"

I squeeze her playfully. "Ha ha," I say, but the truth is, I could eat her entire stash. I'm absolutely starving. And desperate for water. "I guess we should get up, shouldn't we?"

"If we must," she says. "But don't tell Mrs. K I'm keeping this sweatshirt, okay?"

"I'll buy her a new one."

Her grin steals my breath. And then it fades into something

smaller but even warmer. "Thank you for caring enough to fight for me, Nate. To fight *me* for my own safety."

"My pleasure. Not *pleasure* pleasure—"

"Nate," Juliet says. I feel her face lift off of my chest, and when I look down, we lock eyes. She looks heartbreakingly vulnerable, but I've seen how strong she is, too. "Thank you."

I smile.

She smiles.

The world seems to shift as I take a mental snapshot of the moment. Juliet's dark green eyes that can look emerald or hunter, depending on the light. Her long, dark lashes. The little flecks of mascara mingled with her freckles. Her round cheeks and heart shaped face. My beanie on her head, locks of her long hair sticking out.

Her cupid's bow lips, even if they look fuzzy.

Why does everything look fuzzy?

"I should press the button for my floor," I say.

Juliet mumbles a weak agreement. She doesn't sound excited that this night has reached its end, either.

I sit up and rock onto my heels. I stand slowly, holding on to the side rail, and then I press the button for the fifteenth floor. *My* floor.

This night really is over. While she gathers her clothes and bags up the blankets, I bend down to grab my satchel. And the elevator seems to spin.

"Nate!" Juliet cries. "Are you okay?"

I brace myself against the wall. "Yeah, just hungry. And I'm dying of thirst." And my head is foggy and I feel like seeing everything through a dirty window.

"Thirst? You need insulin!" The elevator doors open, and Juliet fits her body beneath my arm as she helps me off the elevator. The whole building is freezing from the power outage. We walk down the hall, Juliet taking a lot more of my weight than I'd have thought possible. When we reach my door—1508

—I fumble for my keys, but Juliet stops me, taking over. She pats my pants pockets, my coat pockets, and then finds them in my satchel.

I feel stupid. This is more effort than anyone should go to for me. I'm too grateful to protest, though. I took my shot last night just before getting out of the car, simply because it used up the rest of my units and I planned to eat soon after getting home. I figured I'd replace what I normally keep in my bag the moment I got to my apartment. I take my insulin with me everywhere, and I've never run out.

Until last night.

Juliet unlocks my apartment door and rushes me inside. She deposits me on my leather couch.

"Lie down," she orders, pulling off my shoes and twisting my body so my feet are up on the armrest and my head is on the cushion. "Where's your blood glucose monitor and insulin?"

"In the bathroom," I say. I'm so tired, and if I don't get that water soon, I'm going to have a nervous breakdown. But I'm too weak for a nervous breakdown.

I'm so weak.

I'm so tired.

"I need to use the bathroom," I mutter.

"Keep that butt on that couch, or I will put you in a coma that makes a diabetic coma look mild."

"What?"

After pricking me to check my blood glucose levels, she must do some quick math, because she swabs the skin on my abdomen, pinches, and injects the insulin like a pro. Then she puts everything back tidily, including putting the used needle in the sharps container in my bathroom. I hear the telltale sound of the needle falling in.

I've dated women who shuddered when they saw me give myself a shot. One woman actually fainted and broke up with me when she came to. If I'd liked her as much as I already like

47

Juliet, I'd have taken it personally, but instead, I was glad. After so many years of trying to prove myself to my parents, I don't continue relationships with people who can't accept me as I am. No hard feelings, ladies. Needles and chronic medical conditions aren't for everyone. But we're a package deal.

I want to get up, but Juliet comes back to the couch to sit next to me and she gives me water, which I drain quickly. She takes the glass from me and sets it down. A moment later, her finger traces my bottom lip.

"Your fat lip has lost weight," she says softly. Tenderly, even.

I smile but can't find words to respond, because her finger running over my mouth has robbed me of my senses.

The next thing I know, her fingertips are skimming over my cheek and up into my hair.

The sensation makes my eyes close, both because of exhaustion and because of how good it feels to have her nails on my scalp. "Mmm."

"Can I get you anything else?"

"No. Thanks, Juliet. I don't know what I would have done without you," I say.

"You would have done jumping jacks or taken the stairs to lower your blood sugar until you made it," she says.

"Or I would have passed out. I missed the signs. I *never* miss the signs."

"You were too busy taking care of me." Her body is perched on the edge of the couch, her hip against my waist. Since last night, her presence has gone from an irritant to a responsibility to a comfort and something more.

"And now you're returning the favor. Thank you."

"My pleasure." She pats my abs. "And I mean *pleasure* pleasure." I chuckle, but my eyes are still closed. "Looks like you're stuck with me for another fifteen to thirty minutes," she says. "If you fall asleep, I'll check your levels again before going, okay?"

"I'm not going to fall asleep."

"Your eyes are closed."

"Because your outfit is embarrassing."

"Liar. You think it's the hottest thing since apple cider. You're rethinking Mrs. Kikuchi as a potential love interest."

I smile. "I'm really not."

"You're in denial."

Her fingers keep running through my hair.

Sometime later, I feel a prick on my finger. Then I hear her voice mingle with my dreams.

"Your blood glucose is good. I'm going to go now, okay?"

I don't want her to go, but I'm too tired to insist otherwise. I mumble something, and then it may be the dream, but I swear, I feel her lips graze my cheek. The click of my apartment door is the last thing I hear before I fall back asleep.

CHAPTER SEVEN

NATE

I don't know what time it is when I hear a voice carrying from outside, but I immediately know it's Juliet. The sun blasts through my open curtains, and I rub my eyes, amazed at how much better I feel.

I stand up and get my bearings. It's ten a.m.

I immediately text my secretary. I don't like taking her away from her family on weekends, but she's got her finger on the pulse of the office. She texts back that nearly everyone is staying home today because of icing on the roads. She assures me I'm safe.

I exhale my nerves. My boss, Terrence, hinted last week that he and the other managing partners are considering promoting me to junior partner. Since then, I've upped my hours considerably. Showing up today would be further proof of my work ethic and give me another leg up on the competition. Normally, this thought would light a fire under me.

But after last night and my conversation with Juliet, the fire is more like a small flame. And it's flickering.

I want to do my best, and I love the law, but being a corporate lawyer is everything the movies say it is: long hours, meetings, and endless paperwork.

I'd love to say hi to Juliet. I'd really love to. But I need a shower, and then I should really go to the office. Also, she's on the phone still, and it sounds like she's talking to Gran. I know well how long she can talk to her grandmother. I'll shower now, and if she's still out when I'm done, then I can debate whether or not to say something to her.

Soon, I'm dressed and ready for the day, with my clothes from last night ready to be taken to the dry cleaner. I can still hear her as I take my insulin, eat, and pack my satchel with more insulin. But the moment she ends her call, I hear her window upstairs slam closed.

She's already back in her apartment.

I missed her.

I try not to let the disappointment derail me. My feet guide me toward the elevator, but I stop abruptly before my finger can press the button.

No, I think I'm done with the elevator for a while.

I turn around and head to the opposite end of the hall for the stairwell. When I open the door, I hear a sharp, "Watch it!"

"Juliet?"

"Nate?"

Excitement flutters in my gut. "I guess I'm not the only one swearing off of the elevator, am I?"

"Ha. Right there with you," she says warmly. In jeans, sneakers, and a cozy sweater beneath her unzipped parka, she looks like she's glowing from within. Although part of me can't help but notice it's a *youthful* glow, a growing part of me doesn't care about her age. Only a handful of hours ago in my apartment,

51

she showed a competence, maturity, and coolness in crisis that people twice her age couldn't display.

We start down the stairs and I ask her where she's off to.

"To go get my hair and makeup done for my sister's wedding. It's at the Windsor, funny enough."

"The same hotel where my parents' party is next week? What an odd coincidence." I don't tell her that my parents own the Windsor.

"My sister's marrying into the Whitley family. Do you know them?"

"Are you asking me because rich people all know each other?"

"Obviously." Our steps echo in the stairwell.

"The stereotypes are true. I went to school with the oldest, Bennett. Which is she marrying?"

"Zach. The youngest."

"Will your family give you a hard time all night about how that could have been you?"

"Oh yeah. It's going to be part of every toast." Her tone is light, but the words carry an edge. I think about the amazing woman I got to know last night, a woman whose brain works differently than her families' brains and who never had a single resource or even discussion to help her understand or manage her thought patterns. The idea of her being the butt of everyone's jokes tonight makes my insides seethe like hot lava.

"Then it's a good thing you're bringing someone even better."

I take two more steps before I realize she stopped. "Are you saying what I think you're saying?" she asks.

"What do you think I'm saying?"

"That you got me a date with Pedro Pascal?"

I throw my head back in laughter. "Wow. It's like that, is it?"

Her smile is so big, and she has her bottom lip in between

her teeth, and I have never felt this way about a woman before. "Would you really go with me?" she asks.

"Gladly," I say with an earnestness I would only admit to under oath.

She throws her hands up and squeals before hugging me around the waist. "You are saving my life! Again!" She threads her arm through mine as we continue our walk downstairs. She's so happy that I wonder if she feels the same way I do. If she's fallen like I have.

"This is perfect! Should I come to your parents' anniversary party with you?"

"Yes. I would be honored."

"Okay, so what's the story?" She squeezes my arm. "When did we meet? What was our first date like? Who fell first?"

I grab the railing to steady myself. "What?"

"Well, if we're fake dating, we need to have a story, right?"

My brow furrows. She thinks I'm doing this for show? "No story. We met last night. And look at you: you're gorgeous, smart, and funny. I obviously fell first."

She swats my hand. "Ooh, good. The best stories are always closest to the truth. So we've seen each other for months in the complex, we've known about each other, of course, but we officially met last night on the elevator and both fell hard and fast. My family will believe it because I go through crushes like bubble gum."

Last night felt like sacred ground, and now she's talking about it like it's a ploy, talking about me as a piece of gum she'll chew up and spit out.

What am I doing? I don't need this distraction. I need to put my head down and focus on work. I'm tempted to rescind my offer when we get to the lobby and find an elevator repairman. Juliet stops just outside the open doors.

"Be good to that elevator, okay?" she says after a pause. "It holds some special memories."

The man looks at her like she's crazy, but I can't help wondering if she's being honest.

By the time we reach the parking garage, Juliet has gone through all the logistics of the evening, and she promises to text me any reminders. She takes a selfie with me and puts it on her phone's wallpaper and then blows me a kiss when I leave the stairwell for my car.

She's leaning into this "fake dating" idea she's made up for herself, but I can't tell if she's being sincere. She was light and bright this morning, but I've seen past her walls, and I know there are layers upon layers that she's hiding.

Or, maybe she isn't interested in me that way.

One thing is certain: her feelings may not be real, but mine are.

And I have no idea what to do with that.

CHAPTER EIGHT

JULIET

"*Y*ou what?" Cousin Lori says in a makeup chair.

"Why are you surprised?" Cousin Lacey says in the chair next to her. "Falling for a guy she met during a blackout while stranded on an elevator is *the* most Juliet thing ever. Right?"

"Classic Juliet," my sister agrees from her chair. Jocelyn speaks with more affection than our cousins do, but I have to wonder if it's for show. Her future mother-in-law is in the room, after all.

It's one thing for my cousins to pile on me. Jocelyn and I are the youngest of the cousins, and our family will pile on anyone if they think it'll get a laugh. It hurts when Jocelyn gets involved, though. When we were younger, it always felt like us against them.

Not anymore.

"It's not like that," I protest. "We were stuck for over six hours, and we've known about each other for months. One of the residents has been trying to set us up since I moved in."

"That's not the same thing as going out on real dates. But I guess if you can't meet a guy the traditional way, why not get trapped in an elevator together?" Cousin Lori asks.

Do I tell her that she's twenty-seven and single, so the "traditional way" clearly isn't working for her, either? Or do I let it slide?

Who am I kidding? I let everything slide.

"Getting trapped in an elevator is so cliché," Lacey says.

Lori and Lacey aren't twins, but they're twice as annoying together as they are apart.

"I think you mean it's a trope," I tell her. "A cliché is something lazy that's used too often. A trope is an established genre archetype."

"What's the difference?" Jocelyn asks.

"A cliché isn't necessarily a story element. Like saying you avoid something like the plague. It's a lazy way of making a point, and everyone says it, so it's considered a cliché."

"So what's a trope?"

"It's a … staple of the genre. Like in a romantic comedy where the leads check into a hotel but there's only one bed."

"I *love* that!" Jocelyn says, and her excitement feeds mine.

"It's so good, right? Although, I really want an 'only one tent' story."

"Ooh, or 'only one *sleeping bag*,'" Joce says. "With some *actual* hypothermia." She raises an eyebrow at me, and I can't help but laugh.

Until Lacey chimes in.

She makes her voice high and mocking. "Or how about only one blah blah blah a trope is an established genre blah blah. Grown women at a wedding gushing about cheesy love scenes? Ugh. *You two* are cliché." She acts like it's gentle ribbing, like she's not mocking me for knowing something she didn't or mocking us for having a conversation where we just enjoy something instead of ripping on it.

I look at Joce, thinking this will be the moment where we regain the connection we had all our lives until the last few years. Joce looks down at her hands, though. Her hair stylist is working on the back of her hair, so maybe she's only being accommodating.

It feels like rejection, though. She and I together could take Lacey and Lori.

But she doesn't want that.

She doesn't want to align herself with *me*.

"Which dropped major did you learn that one from, anyway?" Lori asks, laughing.

I learned it in You Suck 101, I think, but I can't say that because I never snap back when my family is being awful and, more importantly, *You Suck 101* would be a course, not a major. No one else would pick up on that, but the gaffe would drive me crazy.

I bite my tongue and swallow the almost brilliant retort. I smile instead. "You got me!"

The door to the bridal suite opens, and Mom breezes through with a tight smile. "What's going on here, my darlings?" She kisses Jocelyn's cheek and then mine. "Look at my gorgeous girls."

I look at Jocelyn in the mirror, and Jocelyn ... also looks at Jocelyn in the mirror.

"Jules was just telling us about her new boyfriend," my sister says, placing just the right amount of emphasis on "boyfriend" to highlight it without sounding like she's highlighting it.

It hurts.

Lori and Lacey smirk, though, and Jocelyn's eyes jump to theirs. Something twitches in her face. Does that mean relief? Happiness? Whatever it is, Jocelyn was able to poke at me, and it got the reaction she wanted from our cousins. That reaction seems to fuel her. "They were stuck in an elevator during the blackout. Isn't that romantic?"

Does she know she's making a mockery of one of the most special nights of my life?

Does she care?

Mom looks momentarily stunned before smiling at me. "How ... fun! Juliet always finds the most unique way to do anything. Why not choose the most unique way to find a man?"

Do you think I caused a blackout to get a date? I want to cry.

I laugh, instead. I always laugh instead. I smile, I say meaningless things like, "I know, right?" and pretend that I'm fine, because heaven forbid I *prove* that I'm the hard one. My very existence has already proved that. Jocelyn is a full sixty-two minutes older than I am. Her delivery was easy peasy.

Want to guess how mine was?

I feel like I've been paying for it ever since.

Fortunately, Mom notices Mrs. Whitley—Jocelyn's future mother-in-law—and decides to talk to her instead of stepping on me. My cousins, aunts, and sister all follow suit.

And I sit in my chair, feeling the sting of not being enough for my own family.

* * *

After a few hours of my family leaving me alone to talk about other things, I feel a little better. Especially dressed up as I am.

I stand at the top of the ornate spiral staircase outside the famed Windsor Hotel's Grand Ballroom with my cousins. The three of us are dressed in matching ivory chiffon bridesmaid gowns. To her credit, Jocelyn picked amazing bridesmaid dresses.

The bodice is gathered and shows off my waist, while the billowy skirt has a slit that stops a few inches above my knee.

I'm several inches shorter than my cousins, and the slit looks amazing with their height. But I feel beautiful in this dress.

I can't wait for Nate to see me in it.

I'm on pins and needles waiting for him.

At least until my cousins open their mouths.

"Are you sure he's even coming?" Lori asks.

"I'm still wondering if you made him up," Lacey says. "The whole thing was a fever dream from eating too many candy bars."

The two cackle like Macbeth's witches.

"I would do anything to eat a candy bar right now," Lori sighs. "I knew I shouldn't have done the dress fitting before Thanksgiving. I've missed the year's best eating weeks."

Lacey groans. "Seriously, do I have to listen to you talk about your weight again? It's not the 90s, bro. Maintaining a size for a dress is so anti-feminist."

Mom catches my eye and we both roll our lips in to keep from smiling. Lori and Lacey can fight with anyone about anything.

"So is calling a woman 'bro,' sis. And it's not like I *lost* weight to fit into it. I like to give myself padding in the winter and I've missed the chance."

"*Padding?* Do you hear yourself?"

"Do I really have to filter everything I say to my own sister?"

They mercifully keep bickering, and I'm relieved that I don't have to entertain them.

Although, I wouldn't mind getting to brag about Nate a little. It's rude, but I can see why they think I made him up. He's hot. He's European. He's a grown man with a stable job. He can stand up for himself but can also admit when he's wrong. And he's funny! His humor is drier than most people's, but it suits me. I love winding him up, he loves playing the straight man to my goofball, and we work.

He's almost *too* perfect for me.

He was on the elevator, at any rate, when he had no other options or distractions.

Maybe in the real world, it'll be different. Maybe he'll find me obnoxious and tiresome. Maybe I'll find that, even with feelings as colossal as mine are now, he can't sustain my interest. Maybe no matter how hard I try, I won't be able to "keep in the crazy," as Lacey would say.

My excitement quells like a peasant uprising.

Good thing this is all fake.

Ish.

Between you and me, I don't want this to be fake. Nate offering to come with me was the kindest thing a friend could do—and we are friends after last night. More than friends. But when he said he fell first, he was so convincing, *I* almost believed him. My family has been bratty about him, but when they see him, when they talk to him, that'll change.

Nate commands respect in a way I covet but can't fathom.

But if he doesn't get here in two minutes, I'm going to kill him.

I shoot off a text.

Juliet: Where are you?

NATE: Got held up talking to the police.

Juliet: About what??

NATE: You.

. . .

NATE: Because it's criminal how hot you look.

I flush from head to toe.

I drop my phone and look around until I spot him. He's walking up the stairs to the Grand Ballroom.

In a tux.

His hair is pulled back in all its wavy glory, and his beard is trimmed a bit tighter than it was last night.

I didn't know he could get hotter.

I was wrong.

"That must be a friend of the Whitley's," Mom says, because of course anyone who looks like Nate couldn't be here for any other reason.

Lori elbows me. "Now that's a guy I'd want to get stuck in an elevator with."

"You should be so lucky," I say. I wave at Nate, whose eyes are locked on mine. A grin stretches across his face, and he runs up the stairs like he knows my family is a bunch of jagweeds.

Or like he can't wait to hold me ...

I break away from my family, my smile matching his. The slit in my gown comes in handy, allowing me to take a few running steps to meet him. I throw my arms around his shoulders, and he wraps me up in a strong hug and lifts me off the ground.

I revel in the feeling of his arms around me. He holds me like he doesn't want to let go.

"You are breathtaking," he says in my ear.

My heart hammers. "You know, you could kiss me if we really want to sell this."

He growls in my ear. "You want me to sell this?"

He sets me down and stares into my eyes. *It's not real, Juliet. He's just a guy doing a solid for his ... co-survivor.* I nod, even though a kiss would only deepen the emotion, even though my feelings have inched past crush territory and entered a wild, unchartered world.

He brings his face down to mine, his eyes fixed on my mouth. I start to close my eyes, but at the last moment, he moves his lips to press softly, tantalizingly against my cheek. His breath on my face sets me on fire. "I'm not selling anything, Juliet Louise Shippe. Not for them."

A wave of sparks leaves a trail down my body that burns me to a crisp. How is it possible that I was freezing to death last night and am burning alive now? And what is he talking about? He's not going to kiss me, that much is clear. But does that mean he's not going to play along? Did he have a change of heart?

He takes both of my hands and looks me up and down. "Wow, Juliet. I didn't know you could get more beautiful."

"More beautiful than wet hair, a beanie, and a kitten sweatshirt?" I laugh.

"Don't knock the kitten sweatshirt," he says, but he's still looking me over. "*Nossa.* Wow."

"You look pretty hot yourself," I say, running my hands over his lapels like girls do in movies. I get why they do it now. It's a familiar, intimate gesture, but it's also possessive. I feel like I'm staking a claim. And with Lori and Lacey encroaching on our territory, I want to make my claim very clear.

My cousins are beautiful and bold and *not* working on their fifth major in seven years. My mom is about to join us when someone from the wedding coordinator's team comes over and occupies her attention.

"To be clear, are we or are we not fake dating?" I ask through my smile.

"I'm not."

"Enigmatic much?"

"I love it when you talk nerdy to me," he says quietly. "Now why don't you introduce me to these two eager women."

Eager doesn't begin to describe Lori and Lacey. They're

chomping at the bit. I thread my fingers through his and guide him forward.

"Lori, Lacey, this is—"

"Nate Cruz." He puts his left arm around my waist and holds his right hand out to shake theirs. "Juliet's date."

His hand rests on my hip, his thumb grazing my waist through the thin material. My knees go weak at his touch. Does he expect me to be able to walk down the aisle after all this affection? Is he *trying* to sabotage me in front of my family?

My cousins fawn over him, and he shows a polite interest in them that doesn't feel fake but also isn't pushing any limits toward flirtation. In other words, it feels real.

It all feels real.

Mom gets free of the last minute preparations and comes over.

"Mom, this is Nate Cruz. Nate, meet my mom, Janene Shippe."

"Honored to meet you, Mrs. Shippe," he says. He's as smooth as silk but my mom's gaze looks for a snag.

"Nice to meet you, Nate. I was surprised to hear that you two are dating when Juliet just broke up with someone."

I grit my teeth but keep smiling "You can't call it breaking up if we were never together, Mom."

"But *you two* are together?" Skepticism drips from her voice.

Nate answers before I can. "Mrs. Shippe, I know this must seem strange, but do you believe in love at first sight?"

"No."

He laughs. "Neither do I. I've run into your daughter twice a week for six months, and up until last night, every time was an annoyance."

Mom's eyes narrow, almost defensively. "Excuse me?"

"I'm trying to be transparent. We fought for the same parking spot—"

"You're White Prius?" Mom asks.

"He's White Prius," I confirm, smirking at Nate. I forgot to tell him my little nickname. "And he's also the lawyer helping Mrs. Kikuchi. And the one Mrs. Kikuchi has tried to set me up with for months. And the one who kept me safe last night."

"Even when she refused to believe in hypothermia," Nate adds.

"Hypothermia is an excuse for would-be cannibals," I tease, earning a look of annoyed affection from Nate that I want to be real, especially with his arm around me.

Is it real?

Mom's gaze snaps to Nate. "Was she actually hypothermic?"

"No, she was never in danger. We were able to open the doors enough for Mrs. Kikuchi to drop us down blankets and supplies."

"And I ordered a space blanket for my purse so that next time our cheap elevator breaks down, we're both safe." I look up at Nate, "I got you one, too."

"Really?" he asks, and I know the question is sincere by the surprised line between his brows. I became fluent in Nate's face last night.

I give him a small smile just as a wedding coordinator comes over to ask Nate to take his seat.

Nate kisses my cheek, says his goodbyes, and goes into the ballroom to sit. My mom doesn't say anything, but Lori and Lacey can't stop gawking at him as we take our positions.

"I take it all back," Lori says just before walking down the aisle. "I just met him and I'm already in love."

I know the feeling, Lori.

* * *

Somehow I make it down the aisle and all the way through the wedding without combusting every time I look at—or think about—Nate. Which is the whole time. I struggle to pay attention while Jocelyn and Zach give their vows, and I barely tear up when they kiss.

Nate occupies my senses. I can still smell his aftershave—sandalwood and cedar—and I can feel the ghost of his lips on my face.

His supportive, seductive smile carries me all the way through the ceremony and into the reception. We go into the bride's room to touch up Jocelyn's hair and makeup before the reception, and everyone turns on me.

"I can't believe that's the man you were on an elevator with for six hours," Mom says.

She and Jocelyn's mother-in-law adjust Jocelyn's tiara and veil. My mom is an inch taller than Jocelyn and I are, and her curves have twenty-four more years of gravity than ours do, but she's still lovely. She keeps her hair a few inches past her jaw with those finger waves I've never fully mastered.

Mrs. Whitley, on the other hand, has the skin routine and plastic surgeon of a multi-millionaire. She has that ageless look that somehow makes her look younger and older than my mom at the same time.

My aunts and cousins will take their cues from my mom, and Mom wants nothing more than to impress Mrs. Whitley, but something tells me she's shocked enough by Nate's presence to forget that this isn't the time for a public interrogation.

"That's him," I say.

"He looks familiar," Mrs. Whitley says.

I'm about to tell her exactly who he is when my cousins chime in.

"He's hot," Lacey says.

"So hot," Lori says.

"Mom, can you get me some water?" Jocelyn says. My sister is radiant in her dress. We're identical twins, so it's always weird thinking of how pretty my sister is. We're the same size, have the same hair, though hers is a few inches longer than mine and is half up. Her makeup is more glamorous tonight than mine, but even without these minor differences, she carries herself differently than I do. She has the poise of a debutante or a duchess.

I don't.

"I'm thrilled you've found someone you care about, Juliet," Jocelyn says. "What does he do?"

"He's a lawyer," I say.

"And does he ... know what you do?" She looks so innocent, like she isn't suggesting that I'm some kind of an aimless joke. Her quick glance toward my cousins reveals the truth, though.

I'm normally so good at laughing this off. Why can't I now? "Are you asking if he knows I'm a student or if he knows I've switched majors five times?"

"No need to get waspish," Mom says. To *me*.

The unjustness of her reprimand burns in my chest. "I'm not being waspish, I'm being clear. Yes, he knows. Funny enough, it doesn't bother him." Does it? He didn't explicitly say it didn't bother him. If anything, he made it feel like part of my "giftedness."

I felt special last night.

I don't now.

Lacey and Lori swap glances. Mom doesn't say anything.

"You're so spontaneous and fun, and you have a way of drawing in the most interesting men," Mom says. "I hope he'll enjoy getting to know the real you."

As if any of you know the real me.

My family acts like I drive every guy away, but they forget that I'm typically the one who loses interest. If my "crazy" brings all the boys to the yard, it also keeps them there until I shoo them away.

Nate figured out in a couple of hours something my family never has: I put up a front every time I'm with them. I act dumb when I feel vulnerable so I can test people, see if they can be trusted with who I really am. I do it to protect myself. I *am* spontaneous and quirky, but I play it up because it's easier to get criticized for silly choices than it is to be criticized for the core of who I am.

They all think I'm flighty and mercurial, and if it were just about a major, I'd take my lumps.

It's not just about a major, though. It's about everything I've ever done. Every question I've ever asked. Every conversation I've ever taken too far because the need to know their thoughts was like a compulsion. It's about being told no without a reason and everyone expecting me to simply accept it. It's about every time I win at a strategy game or spout interesting facts and they pretend it was a one off.

It's about the fact that I loved nursing school, and they acted like I caused Gran's stroke rather than missing the symptoms. I overheard Jocelyn in the hospital.

What's the point of nursing school if you miss something so obvious?

Overhearing that, overhearing everyone agree, was the moment I realized how my family really feels about me. Jocelyn is the golden child. I'm the imitation knockoff that unravels ten minutes after you put it on.

My front is the only protection I have.

Jocelyn looks at me in the mirror while Mom adjusts the last pin in her hair. "Well, you're one date in, so let's hope it lasts!" Jocelyn crosses her fingers with a cheeky smile.

I should laugh with everyone else. It always makes things easier. The fake smile won't come, though. Instead, words push their way to the tip of my tongue. I'm about to ask her why she has to be so hurtful when she's so universally adored, but the wedding coordinator rushes in before I can. And no one even notices that the wind has been taken from my sails and I'm left alone without an oar.

Except, I *do* have an oar.

Whether Nate is faking interest or not, he's my friend. He could have chosen to do anything else tonight, and he chose to come here and support *me*. And suddenly, not only do I have an oar, I have a strong, steady wind at my back.

I can do this.

The coordinator ushers us into the stunning Terrace Room, where the family dinner and reception is being held. The room looks like it was pulled straight from one of Gatsby's parties (thank you, English major).

We all sit at the head table, and I look around the room until I spot Nate two tables back. He's seated with ...

Gran. My aunts and uncles are there, too, but I warm to think of Nate talking to Gran. Then I rapidly cool. She's never fully recovered from the stroke. She converses fine, but she loses words sometimes and she's not as steady on her feet. Both serve as a constant reminder that if I'd been a better nurse, she'd be okay.

I glance around the rest of the room to see a who's who of socialites in the Whitley's elite world, as well as my extended family and some of our closest friends. The scales are tipped in the Whitley's favor. Did Zach's family insist on taking up most of the guest space, or did my parents choose that to be amenable?

The Whitleys own a dozen of the most upscale restaurants in Chicago. Getting into Le Grenouille is harder than getting into a new show on Broadway. Every celebrity who's anybody has eaten there, and their other restaurants aren't far behind.

My parents own two Chili's franchises.

They've done well for us. Growing up, I always thought they seemed happy with the comfortable upper middle class life they provided us. What was there to be unhappy about?

But then, three years ago, things started to crumble. I let Jocelyn take my place on my date with Zach only a week or two before Gran's stroke. And those two events changed everything.

Before then, my family teased me, but I still felt loved. I may have figured Jocelyn was the favorite, but it went from a suspicion to blue check verified. I went back to school, dated a few duds, and Mom's criticisms amped up. By my third major change, her disappointment was a living thing.

Then when Zach proposed last Christmas, the "That could have been you" comments started piling in from everyone from my parents to my third cousins twice removed. The family even changed the lyrics of a Christmas song, swapping "single" for "jingle."

Single all the way.

That's me.

Sometimes I want to scream, "I'm only twenty-four! I don't have to have everything figured out yet!"

But I'd be accused of histrionics, and things would only get worse.

It's so much easier to laugh with them than have them laugh at me.

I wish I weren't such a disappointment, though. I wish they could see the good I do.

The lighting in the room changes. I brace myself for the toasts to come, hoping Nate's presence will be enough to shield me from the worst of it.

Let the comparisons begin.

CHAPTER NINE

NATE

*J*uliet's Gran is sweet and salty: the best combo. Yet the Shippe family treats her with kid gloves. I assume it's because of the stroke. But she squeezed my bicep when I first sat down and said, "Well, well, well. Juliet always did have better taste in men than Jocelyn."

And that's how we became best friends.

Her words slur a little and her hand sometimes shakes, but she has a lively mind and a spark in her eye that is unmistakably Juliet. With a bit of a Betty White vibe, she's impossible not to love.

Her hand also hasn't left my bicep since I sat. I've kept it flexed for long enough that I'm going to be sore tomorrow.

"How long have you been interested in my granddaughter?" she asks.

"Not long enough," I say. She smiles. "We live in the same apartment complex, so we've been familiar with each other for a long time. We only just got together, though."

"Do you make her happy?"

We both look to the head table to see Juliet's eyes fixed on us. The corner of her mouth twitches up.

"I think so. I want nothing more," I say.

She drops her hand from my arm, but the questions start in earnest.

"What do you do for a living?"

"I'm a lawyer."

"When did you last call your mother?"

"On her birthday last month."

"You should call her more."

"You're probably right."

"How would you treat a server who got your order wrong?"

"Patiently. Servers are people, too. They're people who can spit in my food if I'm nasty, though, so I'm never nasty. But if they don't keep my soda refilled, it'll affect the tip."

"Do you cheat at cards?"

"No, do you?"

"Ha! You'll have to play me to find out," she says.

"I shouldn't admit this, but I used to cheat at Hungry Hungry Hippos by tipping the game board toward me." I only ever played against my parents, and I'm quite sure they knew I was cheating.

"A sound strategy. Do you want kids?"

"Yes. And I'd even take twins."

My last answer gets a big grin.

"Everyone thinks Juliet doesn't know what she wants, but they're wrong," she says. Her words run together. "She knows it when she sees it."

"And what is 'it?'"

"A handsome man who sees her as a complex mathematical equation rather than a carnival attraction."

I look over her lined face and bright eyes. "How do you know that?"

"Because she gets it from me." She winks.

I love this woman.

"And what about nursing school?"

"She told you about nursing school?" she asks. I nod. "It was love at first lesson. It's the perfect career for her. A job where you can never know too much about a body or a person? Perfect."

"She can't get past your stroke," I say. The comment earns me shocked looks from a few members of the family around me, but I pay them no mind. It's not like Gran doesn't know she had a stroke. "Can I ask what happened?"

"It wasn't her fault," she says. "It was just after Christmas dinner, and one of my grandsons brought his new dog without asking. I'm allergic, and my allergies got the best of me. I could barely eat, I was sneezing and sniffling so much. To make matters worse, that blasted mutt climbed up on an empty chair while we said grace, and it took a bite out of the turkey."

"Ooh."

"I was not amused," she says, frowning. "After dinner, I sat in my glider and turned on It's a Wonderful Life. Then I got what felt like a migraine. My vision went blurry. I tried to tell my family, but the words wouldn't come. Juliet asked if I was okay, and I didn't answer. I'm a surly old lady, and I don't think anyone was surprised I wasn't answering. Juliet took the dog out for a walk to give me some peace. She thinks she failed me because she didn't see that my face was drooping."

"How would she even think to look for that?"

"That's exactly what I said. When she got back a half hour later, she saw my face and immediately called 911. She blames herself for the delay, but she doesn't understand that she saved me. She's the only one who looked and checked on me. Everyone else would have let me doze off in my chair. The girl is too hard on herself."

"If she can't be perfect at something, she doesn't think it's worth doing."

Gran taps my hand as the lights change in the Terrace Room. "You get it. You see her."

We both sit back. And the toasts begin.

My heart is already aching for Juliet. It's been attuned to her since last night, but even if it weren't, after ten minutes of hearing her name as the punch line of toast after toast, I'm ready to flip tables.

No single speech has delivered a knockout punch, but the cumulative effect is a series of jabs that are wearing her down, no matter how well she masks it.

Jocelyn learned to ride a bike at four while Juliet was watching the spokes on her sister's tires to see when they would blend. Jocelyn was drawing pictures of houses and people while Juliet would draw a bunch of sloppy circles and lines and say it was a bird's eye view of the neighborhood. When Jocelyn was given instructions, she worked. When Juliet was given instructions, she questioned.

"As if there's more than one way to make a peanut butter and jelly sandwich!" her aunt says during her toast, like this is a roast of Juliet rather than Jocelyn's wedding. But it earns her the laughs she's looking for, and Juliet and Jocelyn laugh along with them.

I want to grab the microphone and yell that, of course there are different ways to make a peanut butter sandwich! Are you putting butter down first? Do you put peanut butter on one slice and the jelly on top of the peanut butter or do you put them on opposite sides? Or—let's get crazy!— maybe a thin layer of peanut butter on both sides with jelly in the middle?

Juliet's mom shoots Jules a glance, and she seems relieved to see her daughter laughing. Can she not tell it's fake?

And it's not just Juliet's family making cracks. Jocelyn's childhood best friend explains that, "Jocelyn is the responsible

KATE WATSON

one, and Juliet is the one she's responsible for." No one laughs more than the Shippe family. At least she makes it about the happy couple in the end, though: "Together, they're perfect for so many reasons, all the way from Type A to Z." She points from Jocelyn to Zach and titters into the microphone. This time, I notice Juliet isn't the only twin looking uncomfortable. Her smile is tight. Does Jocelyn get as sick of these comparisons as Juliet does?

Zach's best friend puts it in bro-speak. "Zach, I couldn't be happier for you, man. We always said it would take a real woman to make a husband out of you. When you first went out with Juliet, we didn't expect much to come of it, but in the end, you settled on the twin who's wifey material."

Jocelyn laughs and raises her glass, and any shadow of sympathy I had for her vanishes.

This chump doesn't think Juliet is wifey material?

(Related: what man can look himself in the mirror after saying "wifey material?")

I look at the woman who's captured my heart, and the hold she has on it tightens. She looks so brave, so patient. She's filling the role her family has demanded her to fill for years, and she's doing it with a smile on her face. It's a fake smile. She's squinting too hard to make it look like she's smiling with her eyes, but I know it's really to squeeze back emotion.

I keep looking at her until I catch her eye. For a split second, she looks heartsick. But she gives me a resigned half smile that screams *What do you do?*

And I suddenly know *exactly* what to do.

Zach's *dude bro* is still talking about Jocelyn being a catch, and because he is who he is, he ends it with a raised glass and the words, "To wifey material."

Words that everyone in the room repeats.

Everyone but me and Gran.

74

I squeeze my fist when I feel something soft touch me. I look down to see Juliet's grandmother's hand on mine.

"Juliet's a special girl. I wish everyone could see it."

"I wish *she* could see it."

She pats my hand, and then I rise.

Juliet's side of the family doesn't know who I am, but Zach's side recognizes me quickly. I make my way over to the microphone next to the head table, and a dozen or so guests hold out hands for me to shake. Zach's older brother, Bennett, nods to me from the head table. He whispers to his mom, who elbows his dad, and soon, the entire Whitley family is looking at me.

Here's the thing you should know about my family.

I told Juliet we're rich, and it's true. But not all "rich" is created equal. The Whitleys are rich. They're among the elite of Chicago. Their combined net worth has nearly eight zeroes.

My family has nine.

Yeah, you read that right.

We're billionaires.

You're waiting for me to say "well, my parents are," right?

No, I am, too. My trust fund alone is probably worth more than the combined net worth of every person in this room. Just because I'm too proud to draw on it, doesn't mean it's not mine.

It very much is.

So yes, I know the exact effect I'm having on the Whitleys as I saunter to the front of a gilded room my family literally owns.

And, boy, do I saunter.

Juliet stares appreciatively at me while her cousins practically drool. I wink at the girl I've fallen for before turning and taking the mic.

"I hope you'll forgive my intrusion," I say, earning an indulgent smile from Mrs. Whitley and a raised glass from Mr. Whitley. "I know tonight is supposed to be about Zach and Jocelyn, but I couldn't help noticing that everyone in the room seems just about

75

as obsessed with my date, Juliet, as I am." I get a hearty laugh from the groom's side of the room. The bride's side has grown wary. "I get it! Juliet is captivating. In the course of the first twenty minutes she and I spoke, I think I tasted the entire rainbow of emotions, everything from excitement to irritation to confusion to fascination. When I realized that she is, in fact, a genius, it all made sense."

I've been looking at Juliet, but I look at the crowd for this next part: "I interned at a school for the gifted after graduating from Harvard, and I quickly spotted all the telltale signs of giftedness in Juliet." I turn to her parents now. "You two know what I mean, of course. The way that she can see patterns and make observations that other people miss, how she thinks in more complicated ways than the people around her." I say this offhandedly, not allowing anyone to disagree without looking foolish.

But I don't want to be tacky. I don't want to take everyone else down a notch.

No, that's not entirely true. I want to take them down a thousand notches for acting like such condescending, small-minded tools.

More than I want to take them down, though, I want to elevate Juliet in their eyes. Let them see how elevated she is in mine. I want *her* to see it.

"Last night during the power outage, Juliet and I were stranded for six hours on an elevator together. I ended the night almost passed out due to complications from Type 1 Diabetes, and only Juliet's quick thinking saved me. I won't go into all the details, but if Juliet hadn't been there last night, I wouldn't be here now."

People stir, lean forward, and cover their mouths. Time to bring it back to something approaching a point.

"The thing is, Juliet and Jocelyn are identical twins. So Zach, I think I know a little of what you're feeling. You're preparing to spend the rest of your life with someone who shares DNA with the woman I've fallen for. If Jocelyn is anything like Juliet—and I hope for your sake she is—I trust that she's amazing. I'm confident you two will have a beautiful life together."

I turn my gaze from the happy couple to Juliet and pull out every ounce of smolder I can muster. "I hope to someday be so lucky."

Juliet looks like her insides have been set on fire. I want to burn with her.

"To Zach and Jocelyn!" Everyone raises a glass and repeats my words.

Instead of returning to my seat, I break protocol and walk over to where Juliet is sitting. I plant my hands on the table and lean across, half-smiling. I wasn't nervous in front of everyone —I never am—but I am a bit nervous now that I'm close enough for her to kiss.

Or slap.

But she doesn't look like she's going to slap me. Her eyes are misty, and she looks like she's fighting back a teary grin.

"You didn't have to do that," she whispers.

"I didn't do it for them, I did it for you."

"Does that mean you're going to kiss me now?" She bites her lip, and it makes me want to bite it, too.

"Nope. That would be for them."

She glares playfully and lets me kiss her cheek.

Everyone claps.

The remaining toasts are worthy of the event after that.

Juliet looks like she's radiating light and goodness through every one.

When dinner is over, the reception begins, and as much as I can see that her family is queuing up to talk to me, I'm more eager to dance with Juliet.

How can she outshine her twin—the bride, no less—so effortlessly?

Jocelyn may look like Juliet, but she doesn't have the same

curiosity. Juliet quirks her head when anyone talks, showing an eagerness to learn or understand or glean insight. Juliet has a natural lightness. When she walks, she almost bounces with that same eagerness to experience something new. And she's so quick to laugh. Jocelyn is, too, but she always seems like she's aware that someone is watching.

She's right. People pay so much attention to both of these gorgeous women that it would be impossible for them to get through life without an awareness that someone is always watching and comparing.

Jocelyn is a pristine, locked diary.

Juliet is an open book, complete with dog-eared pages, a cracked spine, and notes excitedly scribbled in the margin. She's the kind of book whose endless depths a reader could never tire of.

Watching her tonight, being so close yet so far, has been torture.

I get the sense that her inner strength has been hard earned. Her family doesn't seem cruel, but they're inexcusably clueless. They either don't know or don't care that they constantly undermine her.

I refuse to make the same mistake.

After watching her for the last hour and a half, I finally have her in my arms, and I want it to mean something. Juliet beats me to the punch, though.

"I see you've fallen in love," she says.

My hand on the small of her back goes sweaty and my throat catches. "Excuse me?" I haven't been hiding my feelings, but love? That's a little much, especially when I shouldn't pursue her at all. I should focus my time and energy on work. At least until my promotion.

I'm helpless to stop, though.

"With Gran. I knew she'd win you over. She never liked any of my boyfriends. So naturally she loves my fake one."

"Keep telling yourself that," I say in spite of my internal cautions. "I'm going to win you over, Juliet Louise Shippe."

Her green eyes sparkle like emeralds in the low lights. "What are you playing at, Nathaniel Oscar Cruz?"

"I'm going to win you over. That's what."

Did I say that in Spanish? She looks like she doesn't understand me. "You don't need to win me over. We're fake dating. I promise I can make it look real without you going through the effort."

I spin her out, and she flows effortlessly away and back toward me. "If I didn't know better, I'd think you'd majored in ballroom dance."

She laughs. "I did musical theater in high school. Not all of us went to elite schools that teach you ballroom dancing."

"Stop it. Harvard's not that fancy," I say.

She snorts. "I like how you dropped that in your toast."

"You noticed that, did you?" I ask. "You're too smart to keep playing dumb, Jules."

"What do you mean?"

"You're pretending that we're fake dating, but there's nothing fake about how I feel. And I think you feel the same way."

The ambition has left the building.

I repeat: the ambition has left the building.

Juliet eyes me. "Are you saying you'd like to be my real boyfriend?"

"If the position is available, I'm more than up for the job." I trail one finger across the neckline at the back of her dress. Her eyes flutter closed for an instant.

"Tempting," she says. "But my family wasn't kidding during all those toasts, Nate. I go through crushes faster than most people go through toothbrushes."

"So you admit you have a crush on me."

"Of course I do! Have you met you? You're brilliant and

funny and laugh at my jokes. You quote Shakespeare and ask me questions and put up with mine. You're also pretty easy on the eyes, as you well know based on that sexy little parade you did up to the table for your toast."

I grin. "You liked it."

"I loved it. I'm going to find the video so Gran and I can watch it on repeat. Nate, I'm insanely into you. I would date you in a heartbeat." Excitement tightens like a fist around my gut. "But I get tired of *everyone*. I break up with *every boy* I've ever dated. I like you too much to let that happen."

"It's not going to happen," I say. I dip my face down so my beard rubs against her cheek. I feel the goosebumps as they erupt across her arms and back.

"How can you say that?" she whispers.

"Because I'm not a boy. I'm a man."

Juliet purses her lip, holding back a grin, but her eyebrows tug together.

Slow down, Nate. My parents always tell me I overdo every-thing, as if I didn't learn it from them. But they'd be right to say it now. I don't need to jump ahead of myself. I can play this smart. I can and will woo her. And then she can decide if she wants more.

She'll want more, won't she?

"You're right that I've fallen for Gran," I tell her. "Now let's talk about how furious your sister is that you look this much better than she does on her wedding day."

She swats my shoulder, swaying under my lead. "Oh, stop it. She looks beautiful, doesn't she?"

"She does. But there's no contest between the two of you."

She looks at her sister dancing with Zach. "We're identical twins, Nate. Need I remind you that her husband couldn't tell the difference between us?"

"Then he's an idiot. Even ignoring the freckle on your lip

and the one on her nose, you have a lightness about you that she couldn't fake if she tried."

"I think you mean flightiness."

"No." I don't like any distance between us, but I pull back. I don't say another word until she looks at me. "Don't do that to yourself, Jules. Don't you dare let them get in your head. You're not flighty. You're amazing."

"That's one of those words dudes on *The Bachelor* use to describe all fourteen of their girlfriends. It doesn't mean anything."

Oh wow. This isn't her being self-deprecating, this is real. This is the kind of pain that only someone who's never been seen or appreciated can feel.

"It *does* mean something. You being amazing isn't generic, it's specific to you. You think your changes in major have made you flighty, but you don't see how fascinating you are. Your interests have only made you more interesting and more interested in others. How is that a bad thing?"

She doesn't answer. She looks too scared to believe me. Good thing I know how to talk.

"You're witty and sharp. You keep me on my toes, and that's no small feat."

"Did you just make a foot pun? Toes? Feat? Really?"

I grit my teeth playfully. "Obviously," I lie. I didn't make the connection until she said it. "See what I mean? You don't let me off easily, and I like that. A lot." She drops her head, but I caught a smile on those perfect lips before they were out of view. "You can make the best of a bad situation. I can't imagine how crazy I would have gone in that elevator all alone last night. With you there, it became—" The words stop in my throat. How honest do I want to be? How vulnerable do I want to make myself? "It became a night I'll never forget."

She looks up. The twinkle lights all throughout the room

dance in her eyes. "Dang, dude," she says so quietly, I have to strain to hear her. "You are really good at this."

"At what?"

"At being my fake boyfriend."

"Keep telling yourself that," I say. She doesn't know how to take a compliment. Yet another thing that carves a pit in my chest. Maybe this is too heavy. Maybe I'm laying it on too thick. "Besides, I have to make up for being the jerk who always took your parking spot and never stopped the elevator for you."

She leans her head on my shoulder, and I'm whisked right back to last night. The feeling of contentment I had as she lay in my arms, simply inhaling and exhaling, was stronger than any feeling I can recall.

"You had your reasons," she says.

"Yeah. I didn't know how hot you were."

She laughs hard, and the feeling of her shaking and squeezing me is like the sun rising over the cityscape after a storm.

We dance, pressed together as closely as we were last night. I wonder how long it'll take for me to stop comparing the here and now with Juliet to that night in the elevator. I don't want it to become the bar against which I measure every future interaction. I want it to be a springboard.

Who am I kidding? It already is.

I hold her tightly and use my extensive ballroom experience to spin her around the floor. Zach and Jocelyn are an attractive couple, and it's their wedding day. But just as many people are staring at Juliet. She's captivating.

After another few dances, she taps out. "I need to pee like a racehorse."

"Do you have a lot of experience with racehorses that I should know about?"

"Always bet on black," she says.

"I think that's about Roulette."

"Meh, maybe. I heard Wesley Snipes say it in a movie once," she says.

"I don't think you're old enough to know who Wesley Snipes is."

"Whoa, finally getting the age jokes. I wondered when you'd go there." She pokes my stomach. I flex just in time for her to keep poking. And then the poking shifts to a bit of a caress.

"No age jokes. We're seven years apart," I say. "That's hardly a concerning gap."

"Are you sure?"

"Aren't you?"

"You're good with your lips. Words!" she blurts. "I mean words. I have no idea if you're good with your lips. Is that dirty? I'm not even sure what that means. Is it about being able to tie a cherry stem in a knot?"

"I think that would be the tongue."

"I think I need to pee," she says.

"Like a racehorse."

She scrunches her nose and gets to her tiptoes to kiss my cheek. "Like a racehorse. Named Wesley Stripes. He's actually a zebra."

I groan. "Go. Before those awful dad jokes turn you into an old man."

"See? It's all about age with you." She squeezes my shoulders and glides off to the restrooms.

I walk over to my table, where Juliet's mom and an aunt and uncle are sitting with Gran. The older woman smiles at me and pats the chair next to her. "You two looked like you were having fun."

"We were. She is remarkable."

"You two make a fine couple. Like Ginger Rogers and ..." she trails off, her brow furrowed in deep frustration.

One of her kids chimes in. "It's Ginger Rogers and—"

But Gran holds a finger up. "Don't. Don't tell me. It'll come."

And she concentrates on the floor for ten, twenty, thirty seconds. We all know the answer, and her family appears to be in agony waiting for her to come up with Fred Astaire's name, but however frustrated they are, she has to be a hundred times more so. "Fred Astaire!" she says, slapping her knee.

The compliment should have lost its glow with that wait, but Gran is so relieved that her emotion spills into me.

I grin. "Thank you. Juliet is a natural. Did she get that from you, too?"

"No, I have two left feet. More like one since that pesky stroke."

I chuckle with her, but Juliet's mom looks at me like I'm talking about something taboo.

"Mr. Cruz," Juliet's mom says, "why don't we dance?"

I normally wouldn't dance with a married woman, but this is such a "mom" move that I can't say no.

"I'd be honored."

On the dance floor, I hold a hand out for her to take and put my other hand respectfully on her lower back.

"Mr. Cruz—"

"It's Nate, please."

"Nate, help me understand what you're doing here."

"I'm dating your daughter."

"Why?"

"Because of every reason I said in my toast and a million more."

"And you think you know her well enough to be so confident?"

"I can see why you'd ask that. But she and I had deeper discussions last night than I've had with women I've dated for a year."

"Infatuation isn't enough to build a relationship on," she argues. "Some first dates last six hours."

"And some people get engaged after the first date," I say. And then, because I'm annoyed that Juliet's mother has no faith in Juliet's ability to discern between infatuation and interest, I say. "Do you really think so poorly of her?"

"Excuse me?" she asks. "I'm trying to protect her. You're different from other men she's dated. She's never had her heart broken before, and something tells me, you're the one who could do it. I saw how she looked at you, how she danced with you. You're not some crush to her, so if you're playing with *my* daughter's feelings, you need to leave right now."

Whoa. I didn't expect her to go Momma Bear on me.

"Mrs. Shippe, it's obvious you love your daughter—"

"I love her more than anything."

"Then help *me* understand why you let people make her the butt of jokes?"

"What do you mean?" she asks, sounding torn between defensiveness and guilt.

I want to lecture her, but I also don't intend for this to be the last time I ever speak with this woman. "Maybe I misread the room."

Mrs. Shippe frowns. She's a lovely woman, and the lines of regret on her face don't detract from it. "I've never meant to hurt her."

"I believe you."

"She's always been so much more difficult than her sister. She never listened to me until she understood every possible reason for what I was saying. When I yelled at her not to run into the street, do you think that stopped her?"

Oh no …

"No, it didn't. She was hit by a car at three. I watched my baby girl get thrown into the air and spend two days in the hospital for a concussion. That same year, she tried to build a robot and almost stuck a fork in the wall to 'connect it.' We put outlet covers on every outlet, and she spent days learning how to take them out. When she burned her finger on the stove, she didn't stop trying to touch it. She wanted to experiment and see what spot on the dial different household items burned at."

"That sounds scary."

"You have no idea," she says, not meeting my eye. "You can't know how terrifying it is to be a parent. You try so hard to teach your kids everything they need to know, and when they don't listen, you imagine every possible worst case scenario, and in her case, every one of them led to death or ... *dismemberment.* Then at eighteen, they're gone and you can only hope they learned something from you. I know I've been critical of Juliet. I guess I hoped when other people started commenting, something they said might click with her. I haven't handled that the right way."

"Mrs. Shippe, I'm sure you've been a good—"

She shakes her head, her eyes glossy. "Juliet was always so smart and so relentless. When she quit nursing weeks before taking her exam, it felt like a waste of her talent and effort. Then she went back to school and changed major after major. It was like she was putting her hand on the burner again, testing every possible temperature. I just wanted to keep her on a good path. I was never trying to hurt her."

"I believe you," I repeat.

"Did she ... did she really save you?"

"She really did."

"And do you really care for her?"

"I really do."

She nods, not looking at me. "You're different, Nate. Be good to her."

"I will be."

Juliet finds us just as the song is ending, and her mom releases me and throws her arms around Juliet.

"I'm sorry, sweetie. I've been so stupid and so critical. I hope you can forgive me."

Juliet's eyes are saucers as she peers at me over her mom's shoulder. Then she sinks into the hug. "Thanks, Mom."

And then they both start crying.

And people keep dancing around them.

And Juliet smiles at me like it's Christmas morning.

And I know I told myself that it's too early for love, but I think I may be lying to myself. Because the feeling in my heart is too big for any other word.

CHAPTER TEN

JULIET

*M*y mom might never stop hugging me, and my cousins are starting to circle.

She keeps saying sorry, and it's obvious she wants to hash out some real pain right now, but as much as I would have welcomed this conversation yesterday, right now, I really want to go dance with Nate.

She sobs another apology, but I stop her.

"We have time to talk about this another day, Mom. Let's celebrate, okay?"

Mom pulls back, but she keeps her hands on my arms. "Okay, sweetie. I love you."

"I love you, too. Now, can you excuse me while I keep Lori from jumping on my date?"

Mom laughs and I stop Lori just in time.

"My date, my dance."

Lori rolls her eyes, but Nate wears a look of such intensity that it sends a flood of desire through me.

I sigh deeply when he pulls me close.

"Feeling territorial?" he asks.

"I'm not about to let you blow my cover with Lori. She's as big a gossip hound as Gran."

"Gossip hound? Are *you* Gran?"

"Do you ever think about anything other than age?"

"Stop trying to distract from the real point, old lady," he says.

"I hate you." I smile.

"You love me."

"Baby, if I loved you, there'd be a lot less fighting and a lot more kissing."

"False," he says.

I groan. "Did you just *Dwight Schrute* me?"

"It's the superior show."

I laugh, and my pulse speeds up. I love that he makes me laugh. I always feel like I'm funnier than the guys I go out with, and it's such a turnoff. But Nate is *delightful*. There's no other word for it. I could get used to laughing with him.

I already am.

"So you think if we were dating for real," I say, "it would be all banter and no kissing? You're not making a very compelling case for yourself, pal."

He leans in so close, his lips graze my ear, making me curve into him reflexively. "Believe me, if we were dating for real, I'd kiss you so well and so good, *you'd* forget which twin you are. But I'd remind you."

"How would you do that?" I ask breathlessly.

"Banter."

I lay my forehead on his shoulder and laugh against him. His fingers on the small of my back spread, and we sway together until I'm ready to admit that I'm not faking. He kisses my jaw, just below my earlobe, and my legs almost give out.

"Nate," I whisper.

"Jules," he says, kissing my cheek.

"What are you doing?"

"Keeping it real."

I should snort, because that is the cheesiest thing I've ever heard, but the thinking part of my brain has very much checked out. "You're not kidding?"

"I'm a grown man," he says. "Why would I fake date a gorgeous, interesting, fascinating woman when I can *actually* date her?"

"Are you reading a script? How do you keep saying the sexiest things a human has ever said?"

He chuckles in my ear. I never realized how sensitive I am, but Nate's lips have pulled all sensation from every other part of my body and focused it right here, where his breath stirs every tiny hair on my ear, cheek, and neck.

"What if I'm not quite there yet?" I ask, and now I'm breathless for another reason. I already like Nate more than I've ever liked anyone. What if we actually date and I never recover from it when we end?

"I'm here either way. I can wait for you to catch up."

"So we're not fake dating?" I say.

"We are adamantly not fake dating."

"But you're okay if we're not *really, fully* dating?"

"Yet," he adds.

I grin, glad he can't see my face. "*Not* fake dating you is the best choice I've ever made, Cruz."

"That sounds like a double negative, Shippe."

"It does, doesn't it?"

He moves back, holds my hand up, and twirls me out and then back in. His face is intense, but the crinkle around his eyes tells me how happy he is.

Me too, I think.

* * *

The next morning, I wake to a text from Nate.

Come outside.

Discovering that Nate is my downstairs neighbor has been fun. I'll be more thoughtful of how loud I am at night, but during the day, I fully intend to randomly jump or drop my *Complete Works of Jane Austen* loudly on the floor.

Just for fun.

To mess with him.

Because I'm an adult.

I throw on a bra, pull my hair up into a messy bun, and wipe the mascara from beneath my eyes before heading out. It's freezing and snowy outside, but the brisk air always picks me up.

"Morning," a voice says from below me.

We're technically not supposed to hang out on the fire escape in case of an actual emergency, but I figure I can move out of the way if an actual emergency ever happens.

Besides, I love being outside. I love the rush and hum of the city. I love adventure and exploring. My plan was to be an international travel nurse. It combined everything I love: people, exploring, and the human body. Medicine has always interested me, but I knew I'd never be happy as a doctor. I intended to be a nurse for five years, see the world, and then come home and go to school to become a nurse practitioner.

But then, Gran had her stroke …

I blink back the memory and smile at Nate, who's holding a brown bakery bag. The contents of the bag waft up to me, and I moan. As good as the contents smell, though, Nate looks even better in joggers and a Henley. I hope I'm not drooling.

"Mind if I come up?"

"I don't know. I thought we weren't supposed to use the fire escapes."

"You're using it right now."

"Right, but *I* didn't swear an oath to uphold the law."

"And *I* didn't swear an oath to never violate a fire code. Now move it, Shippe. I'm coming up."

I move out of the way, and a moment later, Nate is standing in my fire escape patio, bearing warm, freshly baked goods.

I hold out my arms to hug him when I remember that we're not truly dating. But we're seeing each other. And it's not fake. Also, it feels weird *not* to hug him after spending all night glued together.

We shut the Windsor down last night long after Jocelyn and Zach had already left. My cousins and a few of Zach's friends stuck around, and we ended up playing games until 2:30 in the morning, when the cleaning crew kicked us out.

I sat next to Nate the entire time. I tickled his back, he played with my hair, I played with his hair, he kissed my neck, and our lips never once touched.

It was heaven. Kissing would have really taken things to a new level.

But he insists that he won't kiss me until we're "actually, fully dating," and I insist that kissing would probably help tip me over the edge, so we're at an impasse.

I love being at an impasse with Nate. Every interaction we have is so charged, the sparks are undeniable. The longer we're together, the harder it is to convince myself that my feelings are fleeting.

I've shared more with Nate than with almost *anyone* ever. Even with people pitting us against each other as a kid, Jocelyn and I were close growing up. It felt like us against them. We used to tell each other everything.

But something changed us. Was it the fact that I dated Zach first? Was it the fact that she and the family blamed me for missing Gran's stroke? Both happened in such quick succession that the two events have merged in my mind as the time my life imploded. Whatever the answer, all I know is that she and I haven't been close since.

Which means that I feel closer to Nate than almost anyone. Already.

Calling my feelings for him a crush is like calling a tornado windy.

Playing games last night showed me a new side of him. He's competitive, but not mean. He didn't get angry if someone else won a round, but it was like he evaluated everything they did and everything he did, because he wanted to win.

I want to win, too. Not everyone can handle a competitive partner, but together, we're basically a power couple.

During Charades, we established it was a one-word movie. Then he wiggled his fingers out from his mouth and I immediately guessed *Predator*.

During Pictionary, I drew a sweater with a kitten in a stocking on it, and he said, "Beautiful!"

Hey, he's the one who said I looked beautiful in it.

He called my bluffs in poker. I busted him in "Cheat." And every time, we laughed and touched and flirted.

"It's disgusting watching you lovebirds in action," Lacey said.

"Then you should close your eyes, because it's about to get worse," Nate said as he nuzzled my neck.

And now we're standing on my fire escape and all I can think of is his face in my neck. I flush at the memory.

"You okay?" he asks.

"Fine," I choke out. "Should we dig in?"

"Sure. I know how much you like sitting out here, but if it's too cold, maybe we could go inside."

I pull a blanket from my bench and drape it over myself. Then I pat next to me. He obliges and hands me a lemon poppyseed muffin.

"How did you know?" I ask. And then I add, "About the muffin *and* about me liking sitting out here?"

"You're not the only one who likes to sit on the fire escape. I can't tell you the number of times I've heard you come out."

"What? I always talk on the phone when I come out! Have you heard me talking?"

"How do you want me to answer this question?"

I bury my face in my blanket. "Nate! I've broken up with guys out here! And argued with my mom!"

"And talked to the grandmother I finally met," he adds. "And spoiled a lot of Wordles and Quordles for me."

"You deserved it." I sit up and take a bite of the muffin. "Did I talk about lemon poppyseed on the phone once? Is this how you know so much about me?"

"No, I texted Gran this morning."

The muffin is already tasty, but this bit of information kicks it up a notch or ten.

He

texted

my

grandmother.

I don't think my heart can take more of this man without declaring itself property of Nate Cruz. Cruzville, population me.

"I promise you haven't done anything to embarrass yourself. Even when I thought you were a car-spot stealing, floor-stomping brat, your tone was endearing."

I let the brat thing go, because he has a point. But ... "Floor-stomping?"

"You gotta stop the dance parties in your heels, Jules. You're killing me."

I stick out my tongue. "Good thing I'm so cute."

"Yes, yes it is." He nudges me with his shoulder.

We stay outside for another ten minutes before moving into my apartment. We sit on opposite ends of the couch with our feet tangled up in each other. It's absurdly intimate. Total boyfriend/girlfriend stuff. But it feels natural. Inevitable.

I typically go to my family's house on Sundays, but I'm too

content to move. I'm too happy to think about being anywhere else. For hours, Nate tells me stories from every country he's been to, and I tell him horror stories of waiting tables at my parents' restaurant, like the man who asked me to give my sweater to his wife because she was cold but insisted on sitting on the patio. In winter.

"Why didn't they just go inside?"

"Because she wanted to be outside, Nate. Obviously."

"But she was cold."

"That's correct."

"Okay then," he says, playing *this little piggy went to market* on my toes. "So that's why your gran asked me how I treat servers."

"You can tell a lot about a person based on how they treat servers."

"I'd have tipped you big."

"I'd have written my number on your receipt," I say.

He holds my eye and my pinky toe. Warm tingles spread through my feet, up my legs, and straight to my heart. "You know, this would be our third date. If we were dating."

The comment catches me off guard. "What do you mean?"

"The elevator is date number one. Last night's wedding was number two. Breakfast this morning was date number three."

"Okay."

"We should have dinner tomorrow night."

My chest warms. "Why?"

"Because once I'm back at work, I can't spend all day with you."

This feels significant. We're not dating but we're not *not* dating. I put a fingernail up to my mouth, but I don't let myself bite it. I didn't stop biting my fingernails until I was fourteen, and even now, the compulsion to chomp into my long, manicured nails can get overwhelming.

"Okay," I say. "But we're not dating, so it doesn't count."

Am I imagining his eyes tensing? "Of course. Not at all."

"Neither does the elevator."

"We only cuddled for six hours. Why would it?"

"And you didn't ask me out this morning, you just told me to come outside."

He nods. "True."

"So the wedding was date number one and dinner would be number two. If it was a real date."

"Which it's not," he assures me.

"Exactly."

An alarm on his phone buzzes, and I'm shocked when he tells me it's late afternoon. We've spent the entire day together.

"I have a meeting," he says.

I *cannot* show him my disappointment. "On a Sunday evening?"

"A lawyer's work is never done."

"I don't think that's the saying."

"No, but it's the truth."

He kisses my forehead before he leaves. Is it because he's European that he so freely kisses and embraces me? I miss him the second he's gone. We've talked *all day*. How does time cease to exist when I'm with him?

And more importantly, how can I get more time with my *not* boyfriend?

CHAPTER ELEVEN

JULIET

*W*e go out to dinner on Monday night.

He stops by before work on Tuesday morning and after dinner with Mrs. Kikuchi.

On Wednesday, I'm officially on Christmas Break and Nate once again comes bearing breakfast. This time, it's a homemade breakfast burrito.

"What are you still doing at home?" I ask him while we eat at my table. The day is cold and gloomy. "Aren't you up for a promotion? All the John Grisham novels tell me now's the time to work a million hours a week, find a dead body that your partners buried, uncover a dark web of lies and corruption, and then escape into the sunset with the girl."

"Maybe I'm skipping ahead to the last part," he says. "I took the day off. I need to pick up my suit for my parents' party and thought you'd like to come with me."

"I'd love to. But are you allowed to take days off like that?"

"I lose out on billable hours," he admits, peering at me, "but I don't mind as much as I used to."

SWOON.

"Oh, and I'm getting you a dress, too," he adds.

"You don't need to do that."

"I want to."

"Are you secretly worried I'm going to wear a cowgirl outfit to your parents' party?"

"Obviously. With real spurs."

How can I say no to that?

After breakfast, we climb into Nate's car and head to Neiman Marcus.

I can't believe I'm finally sitting in *White Prius's* Prius. I also can't believe that he drives a Prius when he could drive an Aston Martin or hire a dedicated chauffeur.

"So this is the scene of the crime. So many stolen parking spots," I say.

"You listen to too many true crime podcasts. I'm the victim here."

I punch his shoulder and cross my legs in the passenger seat. "Back to the job: how many hours a week do you work, anyway?"

"About seventy."

"*Seventy* hours a week? Nate, that's not a life."

"No, it's not. The managing partners would typically be unhappy with me for even working fifty in a week, let alone skipping today. But I'm struggling to care lately." He looks ahead, eyes on the road, but I can't help thinking this is because of me. I don't know whether to be flattered or racked with guilt. "Anyway, I had my parents invite the partners to their party this weekend. Each of them would kill to represent my parents' company. Needless to say, they're in a very charitable mood."

When we get to Neiman Marcus, Nate guides me by the elbow (who knew how sexy elbow touches were?!) toward the formalwear section and talks to one of the personal shoppers, a pretty older woman named Martha. Soon, we're getting the red carpet treatment.

A lifetime of seeing makeover movies has prepared me for this moment, and let me tell you, I live it up.

I ask to see everything. I try on everything. All the sequins, all the silk. Jimmy Choo heels? Bring it on.

I probably should protest. I probably should insist that I buy something myself. It's not like I'm broke after Jane & Co. gave me that bonus. But Nate seems genuinely happy getting to buy a dress for me, and I'm not so self-sacrificing that a rich guy spending a thousand dollars on me is going to make me feel guilty.

I look at the price tag on the Jimmy Choos.

Okay, two thousand.

Nate is patient. I try on dress after dress. His approval isn't showy, but it's all the better for it, because when he thinks I look good, it's not an over-the-top expression. He doesn't speak with his hands, like he does when we talk. He communicates in signs I doubt he's even aware of. The widening of his eyes, the slight parting of his ultra kissable lips.

When I come out in a long-sleeve, side drape velvet dress in a deep garnet, he leans forward. "*Nossa,*" he breathes.

He said that at my sister's wedding, and I looked it up when I went to the bathroom. It's Portuguese for wow. Because one language isn't sufficient to express my hotness, I want to tease, but *he's* not teasing. He's not flattering. He's trying to pick his jaw off the floor.

Do I sway my hips a bit extra as I walk to the mirrors?

Yes.

Do I catch him staring at me in a dress that hugs my every curve?

Oh yes.

Do I love it?

Stop asking silly questions.

Nate calls our personal shopper over and hands her his credit card.

I laugh. "You haven't seen the other dresses yet."

"You can get any other dress you want. This dress is a gift for me."

Dip me in oil and set me on fire, why don't you? Because that was scorching hot.

I try on a few more dresses, but nothing makes me feel as confident or beautiful, and I gladly accept the dress. And the shoes. And matching clutch. I stop short of accepting earrings, though, because earrings are for Actually, Fully Dating. And we are not.

Yet.

I change back into my clothes and come out to find Nate holding a suit bag and talking to a tailor. I try not to be too bummed that I won't get to watch him try on suits. Nate doing a suit fashion show would probably make me propose to him on the spot, though, so maybe it's a good thing.

The personal shopper, Martha, brings out my bags and boxes.

"You've done something to Mr. Cruz."

"Why do you say that?"

"I've never heard him talk about another woman, let alone bring one here."

"He's taking me to his parents' anniversary party, so this is just insurance against me looking like a fool."

Martha drops her chin and looks at me over her glasses. "You don't really think that."

No, I don't. So why do I insist on pretending I do?

To protect myself.

Meeting him has felt too good to be true. I'm scared I'm going to mess it up or that he's going to tire of me, so I'm preparing myself for what I fear most.

But if I act like a break up is a foregone conclusion, am I *causing* the breakup?

"I think you know the effect you have on him, and I think you should enjoy it," Martha says. "So I took the liberty of ringing up the earrings, too."

I smile.

I like Martha.

But I bet she gets paid on commission.

* * *

Nate wants to leave after shopping, but I grab his hand and pull him through the department store. Neiman Marcus is the highest end of high end, and their Christmas displays are famous. Elegant piano versions of Christmas carols play over the speakers. In one of the windows is a gorgeously decorated dinner table with mannequins wearing festive outfits.

What happens next is basically a montage of every Hallmark movie in history. I tug him through display after display. I ogle cheery crystal carousels and grab stockings and order him a Christmas tree, because his apartment is a blank slate, and he says yes to everything.

"Look at this huge polar bear butler!"

"No."

Almost everything.

Anything classy and understated gets a yes, at least.

I find an old fashioned music box with a couple in a horse drawn carriage, and I wind it. *White Christmas* plays slowly.

"I love music boxes," I say. "Gran had a Christmas one when I was little. I used to sit by the tree and wind it for hours. It was the most beautiful thing I'd ever seen."

"Does she still have it?"

"No, I took it apart to figure out how it works. I couldn't put it back together again."

Nate picks up the music box. "Now she has a new one," he says. Then he grabs another. "And so do you."

"Nate, they're five hundred dollars each."

"You're right. Should we get your mom one, too?"

I will not let myself cry over how intuitive and caring he is, so I smile and move on. I'm also not going to argue with him about how he spends his money, even if it's on me. To him, buying me a five hundred dollar music box is like any of the other guys I dated giving me a piece of gum.

Wait, no. I do some quick "guesstimates" based on comments he's made. No, that music box is way less than a piece of gum to him. One thousand music boxes would be less than a piece of gum to him.

My word.

The man is beyond rich.

I reach for a tin of gingerbread, but he puts his hand on mine.

"What are you doing?" he asks.

"Buying Christmas treats. Christmas is in four days."

"You don't *buy* Christmas treats, you make them."

"No, *you* make them. I try to make them, get furious, and throw them in the garbage."

"Ah," he says, like he's channeling the wisdom of the ages. "You think you know better than the recipe."

"No," I say. "I just think that recipes should be up for negotiation."

"I know what we're doing tonight."

"What?"

"We're baking gingerbread men."

"You already know how?"

"No, but I like baking. I experiment with recipes a lot because of my diabetes. I've become a rather accomplished cook."

"Ugh," I say as he weaves us to a checkout line. "Of course you're good at cooking. You're good at everything."

"Have you considered that I only bring up the things I'm good at? Why would I obsess over the things I'm not?"

Whoa.

If that's not a perspective shift, I don't know what is.

"What are you bad at?"

"Other than geometry and history? Anything handy. I can change a lightbulb, but my skills end there. I called a plumber once because a fork fell into my garbage disposal and I didn't know why my disposal sounded like it was eating metal."

I grab his arm and laugh. The cashier smiles at us. "When was this?"

"When isn't important."

"Oh my gosh, this was recent."

"Time is a construct."

"Like in the last five years? Two years? THIS YEAR?"

"Laugh all you want. Nothing about my upbringing taught me about garbage disposal maintenance."

"You're lying."

"I wish I were."

"Why didn't you look for a video online?"

"Because you don't know what you don't know."

I laugh hysterically. "This is a better gift than you saving my life. Tell me everything."

The entire drive home, he tells me the things he never knew. He didn't know what dangling fan pulls did until he was twenty. He had never plunged a toilet until he moved to our apartment complex.

"The pipes couldn't handle the toilet paper," he says when he realizes the implications of his confession.

"Babe," I say. "Everyone has clogged a toilet."

He smirks. "Babe?"

My cheeks flame. I called him *babe*. Who am I? I've never had a pet name for anyone before. "You're glomming on to 'babe' and not the fact that I admitted to clogging a toilet?"

"Stop trying to change the subject."

We park in the garage and bring our bags in. *Santa Baby* plays in the lobby, and management has put out poinsettias and strung Christmas lights around the elevator, as if to detract from its metal death trap vibe. We wordlessly head for the stairs. As fond as my memories of the elevator are, I don't trust that thing.

Nate's phone rings while we trek up, but he'd have to drop everything to reach it, so we just climb and climb. After days of taking the stairs, you'd think I'd be more used to it. I'm not. This is miserable enough to make me want to never skip church again, if you know what I'm saying. We pause to catch our breath more than once, and I'm gratified that even Nate is panting by the time we reach the fifteenth floor.

It doesn't help that he's holding about twelve shopping bags.

I'm completely out of breath when we reach 1508. As soon as he opens the door, I drop the bags and fall onto his dark leather couch. My lungs and thighs are burning. "I'm never moving again."

Nate puts his bags down and sits on the couch next to me, breathing heavily. He lifts my legs over his, and he puts his hand on my knee while my chest heaves dramatically.

"Does that mean I'll have to decorate all by myself? I guess I could call Lacey or Lori. They both found my LinkedIn profile."

I snap up. "They did not. Did they?" He nods.

Those snakes.

After a two minute breather, I start decorating while Nate pulls out ingredients.

His apartment has the same footprint as mine, but it's so much *nicer*. The furnishings are high end and it's been painted a shade that I can only describe as "richer than you."

"What is Christmas like in Europe?" I ask.

"I like it better there," he says. "Especially Spain. It's less commercialized, and there's no focus on Santa."

"Do kids not get presents?"

"They do, but they're from the Three Kings—the Three Wise Men—not Santa Claus. The gifts don't come until January. The Kings show up as part of a big parade in each town."

I've finished decorating and sit on the opposite side of the island from him as he starts telling me about another Spanish tradition: the pooping Christmas log.

But his phone rings again before I can pepper him with questions about the *pooping Christmas log*.

"Excuse me, I need to get this," he says.

He walks into his bedroom, but I hear him say, "Hi, Mr. Keaton," before the door closes.

I don't eavesdrop, but I want to. I light the citrus clove candle I made him pick up and breathe in the heady scent while I wait.

The call only lasts a couple of minutes, but Nate is visibly frustrated when he returns.

"Everything okay?"

"It's nothing," he says. "Ready to make some gingerbread?"

Whoa. I haven't seen this side of him. The side that freezes or shuts people out. "Was that your boss?"

"Why do you ask?"

"You said 'Mr. Keaton' as your door was closing. It was the only thing I heard, but you didn't sound happy," I say. He frowns. "Don't tell me anything you don't want to tell me, but if you're serious about *not* fake dating, isn't this the kind of thing we'd discuss?"

Why does my heart hammer to say this to him? Is it because I'm playing my hand? It's practically telling him *I want more.*

But Nate isn't convinced. "*Not* fake dating isn't the same as dating. Is it?"

The corner of my mouth quirks up, but I wait. As much as I love bantering with him, I want him to answer the question.

"That was Robert Keaton, one of the managing partners. I don't report to him, but that doesn't stop him from giving me his work." He rubs his hand across his forehead.

"He's giving you *his* work? Don't partners have their own associates? Why would he give his work to another partner's associate?"

"Because he can, and because I'm the best."

"Why do you put up with it?"

"That's how law firms work. He holds all the cards."

"You don't have to work there, though."

He exhales through puffed cheeks. "I want to prove myself."

"To whom?"

Nate's brow creases and he doesn't answer. I want to keep prying. This conversation is a peeling piece of pleather on my steering wheel, and I want to rip it off and see what's underneath.

We were so open in the elevator that it's hard to remember that it wasn't real life. It's different being stuck in a metal box with poor lighting, cuddling together under blankets. Even though we were reasonably sure we were safe and would get out before anything bad happened, there was an element of danger that made self-disclosure so much easier.

There was also the sheer boredom. What would one do for six hours without baring one's soul to a hot nemesis turned crush?

He doesn't have to tell me everything right now. I can tolerate a bit of curiosity. If I have to.

I come around the island and look at the recipe on his screen. I grab a measuring cup and dip it in the flour when his hand stops mine.

"What are you doing?"

"Mixing the dry ingredients."

"You can't just dump flour into a bowl. You have to weigh it."

"Did you just make that up?"

"No. If you can't weigh it, at least scoop it into the measuring cup with a spoon to make it more precise. Packed flour changes the recipe more than you'd think."

I love his hand on mine, so even though what he's saying makes sense, I look over my shoulder at him.

Romantic comedies always have scenes where the guy is showing the girl how to golf or bowl or whatnot, and there's that moment where the girl peers over her shoulder and the guy's face is right there, and they look at each other's lips, and it adds all this delicious tension.

They don't even know.

My breath quickens, while Nate's slows almost to a stop. It was one thing to flirt at the wedding in front of my family. We were playing it up. But here, there's no audience, no one for me to pretend we're pretending in front of. It's Nate and me and a host of real emotions, half of which I couldn't name if I wanted to.

Nate thinks he wants a real relationship with me.

And I'm realizing how much that scares me.

"I take back every bad thing I said about baking," I whisper, looking at his lips.

Nate smiles and leans back just enough to break our contact. How does he do that? How does he read when I'm too over-whelmed? Or did my comment provide the distraction *he* needed to stop himself from jumping in further than he wanted to?

"In that case, let me teach you the ways of the kitchen."

Yes, please.

CHAPTER TWELVE

NATE

I'm glad Juliet didn't push about my work.

I'm disappointed we didn't kiss.

Not fake dating is getting complicated.

When we finish baking and decorating the cookies, we go up to Juliet's apartment and grab festive paper plates, red cellophane wrap, and green bows. We wrap the cookies and then deliver some to our neighbors, the apartment manager, and to Mrs. Kikuchi. Because it's a Wednesday afternoon, most people aren't home, but Mrs. K is.

She invites us in, and she wants details. Lots and lots of details.

"I knew you two would be a perfect fit!" she says. She's wearing a lounge suit and sitting happily in her glider while we sit across from her in the loveseat.

My arm rests on the back of the couch behind Juliet, not quite touching her. Is it a test? Yes. And I don't know if she passes or fails, but she leans against me. She insists that we're not dating, but she touches me so often, I wonder if she knows she's doing it. It's like she can't *not* be physical when I'm nearby.

I'm not complaining.

But it makes her insistence that we're not together harder to swallow.

It hasn't even been a week, I tell myself. *And you're the one who keeps lying to yourself that work should be your priority.*

"You call this 'not dating?'" Mrs. K laughs. "Hon, you don't know what you don't know. You've made this boy play hooky from work. He's never done that for a girlfriend before."

Juliet looks at me slyly. "Has he had a lot of girlfriends?"

Mrs. K shrugs her slight shoulders. "A few. He dated one girl for a year, but they broke up shortly after Jin died. He hasn't dated anyone seriously since then." Mentioning her husband puts a wistful look on her face.

"Does he get serious with every girl he dates?"

"He's sitting right here," I say. "And I don't date a woman unless I think we have potential for more."

"You mean you don't date them unless they're compatible with your work," Mrs. K says. "You've always chosen work over girlfriends. It's nice to see you choosing the girl, for once."

I don't know what effect this is having on Juliet, but I know the effect it's having on me.

I *am* choosing Juliet over work, even when I'm *at* work. I'm distracted by thoughts of her, eager to see her next. I text her throughout the day, something I've never done with another girlfriend.

A foreign weariness overtakes me. I have never dreaded work before. After talking to Robert Keaton today, I called my boss, Terrence, and told him I'd need time off until after the holidays.

As in January.

Associates at firms like KKM don't take time off for the holidays, let alone ten days. They definitely don't take time off when they're up for a major promotion. I hoped securing invitations to my parents' party would be enough to get them off my back. Terrence was surprised, but he wasn't a jerk about it.

Robert and his dad, Bruce, are going to be massive jerks about it.

Everyone in the office will be. This is hardly the time to take a vacation. Now is the time to put my nose to the grindstone, to show them exactly what I'm capable of, not because of my last name but because of *me*. Because of what I bring to the table on my own.

Last Week Me would shake Current Me silly.

Last Week Me was an idiot who didn't know how much more to life there is.

I can't seem to muster up concern for work anymore. Don't get me wrong: I want to work. I love the law. I love justice. But working corporate law is hardly the best way of showing that love.

For the first time since I graduated law school, I wish I were doing something in law that had meaning and that allowed for balance.

Mrs. K has pointed out the obvious: I've never dated a woman who made me reevaluate my life and my priorities.

If Juliet doesn't want to be with me in the end, her life will remain unchanged. Mine won't. I don't know how to go back to contracts and paperwork and finding loopholes for the next forty years when Juliet has made me want more.

We stay at Mrs. K's long enough for a rousing game of scrabble, and I narrowly win when I'm able to convert Juliet's "juke" into "jukebox."

Juliet gasps. "You punk! You've been holding onto 'box' this whole time?"

"Don't hate the player," I say, but she glares anyway.

She's feisty in games. I'm competitive, but she takes it to another level. After the wedding when we played games, she jumped up and did little dances or pranced around, rubbing it in people's faces.

It's not the most attractive thing about her.

But I *like* it. I like that she has flaws and that I can see them without them being a turnoff. I'm not putting her on a pedestal because she's hot and fun. That's obviously what attracted Zach to her in the first place, and attraction is important. But looks fade.

Mrs. Kikuchi and her husband were married for fifty years before his fatal heart attack. I've seen photo albums of them in their earlier years, and they were both attractive people.

But attraction didn't keep them together when it took them twelve years to finally get pregnant. Attraction didn't carry them through the grief of their eldest son dying in a car crash. What good was attraction when they almost went bankrupt or when Mrs. K needed a hip replacement? Or when she left the cap off the toothpaste or when he wouldn't put a new roll of toilet paper in the holder?

I'm not blinded by Juliet's beauty. Her victory laps are tacky. And I can live with that.

Around dinnertime, we leave Mrs. Kikuchi's, as her son and his family are coming by.

"I was thinking of ordering dinner from the Indian place down the street," I tell her. "Want to join me?"

"Okay, but afterwards, can we watch Christmas movies and eat popcorn? Gran and I coordinate our Christmas movie watching schedule. I don't want to miss one."

"Anything for Gran," I say.

"You say that now, but this will be the cheesiest, most delightfully festive romcom you have ever seen. I think it's about a matchmaking Santa puppy who wants his grumpy owner to fall in love for Christmas."

I blink, trying to process her nonsensical words. "Why?"

"Why what?" She laughs.

"Why would someone make that movie?"

She holds out her hands and I take them. We push and pull on each other's hands like a couple of teenagers.

"Because it's about a matchmaking Santa puppy. What's your confusion here?"

"The matchmaking Santa puppy."

"Yes?"

"No."

"No what?"

"No to the whole thing! It's a matchmaking Santa puppy! Does he talk?"

"I hope so."

"I take it back. You're uninvited." I push her away, but our hands are still clasped.

She pulls me in. "Too late! No take backs."

She bounces on the balls of her feet, gives me a kiss on the cheek, and says, "But I'm going to go upstairs and change into PJs."

"It's six p.m."

"Exactly. My restraint all day has been heroic."

"In that case, I'll leave the window open for you to come down."

Twenty minutes later, I've checked my blood glucose, given myself insulin, paid the delivery guy, and changed into pajamas. When I come out of my room, Juliet is already at my table pulling the cartons of food out of the bag.

One leg is tucked under her butt, and I take a moment to watch her. She's washed off her makeup and braided her long blonde hair. She's wearing leggings, boot slippers and Mrs. K's cat sweatshirt (Mrs. K insisted she keep it).

Affection swells in my chest.

She isn't just gorgeous, she's *cute*.

Never in my life have I considered that *cute* could trump

gorgeous, but it does. Beauty is just something that happened to her. Cute is who she is.

"I never realized I was so high maintenance," I say when I join her at the table.

"You have medical needs. Speaking of which, it's time for you to get a continuous glucose monitor so you don't miss the signs ever again. We're calling your doctor tomorrow to get that set up."

"Are we?"

"We are."

A pleasurable swirling sensation swirls in my gut. She couldn't sound more like a girlfriend if she tried.

"As for how much faster I am than you getting ready, have no fear. The older I get, the longer my skin routine will get. I'll be doing face yoga and using retinol in no time."

She acts like it's a throwaway comment, but she said "have no fear."

Like she's warning me that one day, her routine will take longer.

She would only do that, though, if she thinks I'll be part of that future.

I smile and eat. Juliet works at a different speed than I do.

Whether she knows it or not, she's catching up.

CHAPTER THIRTEEN

NATE

J don't know how many more reveals I can handle with Juliet.

On Friday night, two days before Christmas, I pick her up at her apartment. She's wearing the dress I bought her. It's a deep red long sleeve dress that stops at her knees and hugs her curves so tight, I'm jealous.

I'm jealous of a dress.

The Oscar de la Renta crystal drop earrings I asked Martha to box up compliment her blonde waves beautifully, but it's the simple, thin gold necklace she's paired with the outfit that has me fixated. Does she have any idea how sexy her collarbones are?

"I don't think I can keep seeing you like this."

She puts a hand up to her throat. "What? Why?"

"Because not kissing you is the hardest thing I've ever done."

She beams and holds out her hand.

"If you want to say yes to my fake dating proposition, I'll let you kiss me whenever you want."

I take her hand and we walk over to the stairs. "We both know you don't want that."

"Do we, though?"

"Fine. We both know *I* don't want that. Not if it's fake."

I hold the stairwell door open and she puts her hand on my cheek. "You drive a hard bargain, Cruz."

My cheek tingles where her hand was.

After a quick drive where we fight over whose playlist to listen to, we're back at the Windsor for my parents' anniversary party, and nerves cramp my stomach.

I take Juliet's hand, threading her thin fingers through mine. "Thanks for doing this with me."

"Thanks for inviting me."

I want to kiss her hand, but I'm dangerously close to confessing that I love her as it is, and I don't want to scare her away. I nod, instead.

"What am I in for?" she asks. "Are your parents and their friends going to be rude? Will I need to rescue you like you did me?"

"No, very much the opposite. I'm not allowed to have flaws. They'll expect me to be the perfect, dutiful son. They'll want me to impress their friends. It's going to be an evening of talking about Harvard and the rowing team and now being on the partner track with KKM."

"You rowed at Harvard?"

"Only for two years."

"Oh, only two years, huh?" she teases.

"Point is, tonight is going to be nothing but schmoozing and charm."

"Sounds exhausting," she says.

My first instinct is to be defensive. I'm fully aware of my privilege. Her family treats her like a punching bag while my family hoists me up like a museum display. I'm sure she'd love to be treated the way my parents treat me. She'd probably kill to be in a room full of people who see nothing but her accomplishments.

"It's not a big deal."

"Of course it is. You don't even get to be real around your own family. They expect you to be superhuman. You can't have flaws or struggles? How are you supposed to connect with people if you have to be *on* all the time?"

"You're never *allowed* to be on," I counter.

"Are we arguing about why the other person has it harder?" Juliet asks.

"We argue about everything else. Why not this?"

Juliet smiles. "Nate, how can I make tonight go well for you?"

"Just be there."

"I can do that."

* * *

In spite of the lowered lights, everything in the grand ballroom gleams, from the dripping chandeliers to the wine flutes to the server's trays. My parents' guests glitter and sparkle at least as much.

"You ready?" Juliet asks, her arm linked through mine.

"It's show time. Don't judge me for the person I'm about to become."

"Wait, who am I supposed to be?"

Shoot.

I didn't think about that.

People are going to expect Juliet to dazzle as much as I do. What do I tell her to do? Honesty will lead to scrutiny and judgment, and she's had more than enough of that. I don't want her to be anyone other than who she is, but I'm acutely aware that the people in this room don't see value in someone whose resumé doesn't include an Ivy League degree.

"Juliet—"

But I don't get the chance to say anything, because my parents have already spotted us.

My mom and dad glide over to us, looking radiant, as always. We give *besos*—kissing one cheek and then the other—and then they greet Juliet the same way. She's only flustered for a moment, but she adapts quickly. I should have prepared her for this. I spent so much time worrying about how I'd feel that I didn't think about the situation I'm putting her in.

How could I be so selfish?

"Mom, Dad, this is my ..." Panic rolls through my gut. I look down at Juliet, who gives me an arch look. She's not letting me out of this, and somehow that challenging look galvanizes me. "This is Juliet Shippe, the woman I'm desperately trying to make fall in love with me."

Dad laughs. He's every bit the distinguished Spanish gentleman, and even in his mid-fifties, he turns heads. His accent is close enough to Antonio Banderas' that women frequently swoon over him.

"A woman who knows her worth makes a man work for her attention," Dad says, taking Juliet's hand. "I'm Alberto Cruz. It's a pleasure to meet you."

Dang it if Juliet doesn't blush.

Mom puts a hand on Dad's arm. "Mariana Cruz. What a treat to see Nate smitten with a date instead of being bored with her."

"Mom," I say.

"What? It's true." Mom is the more expressive of the pair. Her Portuguese accent is milder than Dad's Spanish. "They're all lovely, I'm sure, but your breakups have seemed more like business arrangements than matters of the heart."

"Nate hasn't told me much about his exes," Juliet says.

117

"Why would I waste a second talking about other women when I'm with you?"

I hold her gaze, and her demeanor softens and warms. "That was a good answer."

Dad chuckles and pats my back. "It's good to see you, son. Let's go greet our guests."

Mom links her arm through Juliet's, and I hear her compliment Juliet on her dress and earrings, and Juliet repays the compliment, and all I can do is try not to worry what they'll think when they find out she's a twenty-four-year-old college student.

Dad and Mom are masters at mingling. It's an art form I'm adept at, but they're elite level pros. It's the little things like giving someone their full attention, touching someone's elbow while they talk, or a well-placed compliment. They ask questions at the right times and stop at the right times, too. They have an ability to guide a conversation exactly where they want it to go.

It's manipulation at its finest, but at least the people they manipulate don't seem to mind. If anything, they feel special.

Heck, everyone in this room feels special. They're on the Cruz's shortlist; how could they not?

"Your parents are amazing," Juliet says in my ear.

I love how we keep finding ourselves at events where we have to get close to speak. It makes every conversation feel intimate.

"They're good at what they do, no question."

"Explain?"

"They're manipulating people. They know how to make people feel good, so they do it."

She mock gasps. "What villains."

"Easy, tiger."

"Why manipulate people? To what end? They're probably some of the richest people in here."

"They're definitely the richest. Well, Jerry may be close," I say, pointing to the owner of one of Chicago's biggest sports teams.

This takes her by surprise. "Seriously?"

"You haven't looked my parents up?"

"Why would I? You told me you were well off."

"We're beyond well off."

"Then that makes my question all the more pertinent: what do they stand to gain by making the rounds like this?"

"Power. Influence. Status."

"All of which they already have."

"True," I say. "But there's always more to accomplish."

Juliet takes an appetizer from a server, her eyes fixed on my parents a few feet away. "That's disappointing. They seem so sincere."

"Like I said, they're good at what they do."

"What was that like for you growing up? Were you not close?"

I cast my mind back to dinner party after dinner party. My dad's hand on one of my shoulders, my mom's on the other. Them listing off my accomplishments, asking me to say something to whatever VIP they were schmoozing. When I said my part, they'd pat my back and send me on my way, and I'd sit at a table in the corner until they called on me again.

Every night at dinner, they asked about my day, and when I didn't know how to answer, they'd get specific. How was school? What was I learning? How were my grades? How did I feel about them? Who was I hanging out with? Was I being a good example to the other kids? Did I represent the Cruz name well?

When we traveled, my parents pointed out everything. They had me look at people and try to assess what I saw. What was going on with them? What were they feeling? When I was scared to order at a restaurant, they refused to help me. Same

119

thing at stores. I was pushed to do things outside of my comfort zone constantly, and while some of that is healthy, their expectations were so far beyond healthy pushing, it was exhausting. My life felt like a constant test of becoming, and I never knew my grade or even what their rubric was.

Juliet's questioning gaze should prompt me to answer, but instead, it keeps me in my past. As demanding as it was, my childhood wasn't affectionless. I remember my mom singing me to sleep and my dad carrying me in after a long flight. I remember them cheering so loudly at my rowing events, I heard them over the splash of the oars and the wind in my ears. They threw me ornate parties, and I went *everywhere* with them, even when it meant bringing tutors with us.

"They cared about me," I say. "It was tiring, but it wasn't bad."

I want to say more, but Jerry approaches my parents, and I guide Juliet forward so I can introduce her. He and my parents catch up for a minute before he turns to me. "And how are you, Nate? How is KKM working for you?" Jerry asks. He's been a family friend for years, and I've watched more than a few sporting events in his box.

"I'm good, sir. Work keeps me busy."

"Not so busy that you neglect your lovely friend, I hope?" he asks Juliet.

"No sir," she says, totally starry eyed.

"I think someone is star struck," I tease.

"Then the four of you should join me in my box for the New Year's game."

Juliet looks like she's going to faint on the spot. "We'd love that, wouldn't we, babe?"

"Anything that makes you call me *babe* gets a yes from me. You're a good wingman, Jerry."

"Yes, well done," Dad agrees. "We're fond of anyone who makes Nate leave the office every now and then."

Behind my parents, I spot Mr. and Mrs. Whitley. They seem

to be sizing everyone up, and I get the feeling they like when the power dynamic is in their favor. They like being the wealthiest people in the room. Here, they're small potatoes.

They wave to me, and I use the manners my parents drilled into me, greeting them like we're old friends.

"Good to see you both," Juliet says, hugging Mrs. Whitley and shaking Mr. Whitley's hand.

A couple shifts behind them, and I catch long blonde hair and sparkling emerald eyes.

It's Jocelyn and Zach.

Jocelyn and Zach?

Juliet looks stunned as Mrs. Whitley introduces everyone.

"I thought you guys didn't get back from your honeymoon till tomorrow morning. What are you doing here?" Juliet asks, giving Jocelyn the briefest of hugs.

Jocelyn's smile is blinding. "Zach's mom got us an earlier flight so we wouldn't have to miss all the family parties. Isn't this a fun surprise?"

Juliet looks like she's going to be sick.

Meanwhile, Mrs. Whitley is talking to my mom. "Thank you for adding Zach and his new bride to your list."

"My pleasure, Sandra. As soon as you told me the connection between our sons and their significant others, I was eager to meet them both."

Mom smiles warmly at Juliet, whose smile is so strained, I wonder how Mom misses it.

I shake hands with Zach, and Jocelyn goes in for a hug. It makes sense for her to do it—I'm dating her sister and went to her wedding—yet it also feels like a power move.

This should be a nice evening for Juliet. She should be able to shine without being in the shadow of her twin, but Jocelyn is talking to Jerry now, charming him, securing an invitation to his box. She speaks freely about her Master's in accounting and job, and soon, she has all eyes on her, monopolizing the conversation without being over-the-top, and garnering praise and compliments left and right.

And Juliet's light keeps getting dimmer and dimmer.

No matter how dim she gets, though, she will always outshine Jocelyn. Her twin is stunning. I know this objectively, because she looks like Juliet. But she has a permanently pinched look that detracts from the beauty her sister naturally radiates. I'm glad I insisted on getting Juliet a dress, shoes, a clutch, *and* the earrings. I only wish I could also put a ring double the size of Jocelyn's rock on Juliet's finger, just to show her who the superior twin really is.

Wow. That's petty of me.

I stand by it.

And I hold Juliet closer, hoping to instill my faith and confidence in her. Meanwhile, her sister elbows in on a night that has absolutely nothing to do with her.

CHAPTER FOURTEEN

JULIET

*J*ocelyn belongs in this room.

I do not.

After she answers every question Nate's parents and Jerry ask, they're all clearly impressed. She has a master's in accounting and works for one of the biggest accounting firms in the country, for heaven's sake.

Jerry tells the Whitleys how accomplished their new daughter-in-law is and then turns to me. "Juliet, I didn't catch what you do."

"I'm studying economics." I try to say it brightly, but I sound as small and insignificant as I feel.

"Wonderful subject," Mr. Whitley says. "We don't see enough women getting advanced degrees in economics."

Wait a minute.

Why would Zach's dad say that? He was at Jocelyn's wedding and heard everyone talking about me and my college status. Was he not paying attention? Or did he do that on purpose?

"I'm still in my undergrad," I say, hating how hot my face feels. "It's taken me longer to find what I love to do."

I look at my sister, who swaps a quick look with her husband. Nate's hand shifts on my hip, surprising me. I forgot he was even next to me, let alone holding me. Jocelyn's presence has made me feel isolated. Adrift at sea.

"So you've changed your major a few times," Jocelyn says in a voice that probably sounds supportive to everyone else. "You'll find it eventually. And in the meantime, you're becoming a jack of all trades! You're the most interesting person at every party." She smiles big, like she didn't give the most backhanded of backhanded compliments.

My throat swells, and the back of my eyes sting.

I hate her.

No, I don't hate her.

I hate myself compared to her.

Isn't it enough that she's married, has two degrees, and is settled in her job? Can't she content herself with having everyone love and admire her? Does she also have to grind me in the ground at the same time?

I want to go. I don't want to be here anymore. Before I can pretend I need to use the restroom, Mrs. Cruz turns to face me. She puts her back to my sister and the Whitleys, something I haven't seen her do yet. Mrs. Cruz has a way of making everyone feel included all the time. I notice she hasn't boxed Jerry out, though.

"Juliet, you are a girl after my own heart," she says in her lightly accented voice. "Did Nate tell you I dropped out of college after my third change in majors? Alberto and I got married my sophomore year, and I was pregnant with Nate by the end of my junior year. I said I quit because of the morning sickness, but the only thing I was sick of was school."

"And I was in law school when I realized how boring I found

it," Nate's dad says. "I was twenty-five, broke, married with a kid, and I had no idea what I was going to do."

"Really?" Nate asks. "You guys never told me this. I thought you were both born with commercial real estate licenses."

Jerry laughs at this. The Whitleys—including the newest Whitley—also smile. Tightly.

"We lucked into real estate and managed to secure loans to make some risky investments that could have gone either way," Mr. Cruz says, "But it all worked out in the end."

"That's what we call an understatement, kids," Jerry says. He doesn't seem to look down at me for not being as successful as my sister. His kindness almost makes the Whitleys' intentional shaming worse.

Most people *aren't* as nice as this man. Most people don't go out of their way to normalize an aimless college student's experience like Nate's parents.

Most people want to compare their successes to my failures so they can buoy themselves up.

Jerry looks around, and we all realize there's a crowd around us, no doubt listening to Nate's parents' story.

"I've monopolized enough of your time," Jerry says to Nate's parents. "See you all next week at the game. And good luck in econ. My friend is the President over at Loyola, so call me if anyone gives you any grief. We'll get it straightened out."

His words make me want to cry with gratitude.

Mr. and Mrs. Whitley follow Jerry's cue, thank goodness, but Jocelyn holds back with Zach as three men make their way toward Nate and his parents.

Why can't she just leave? She's standing so straight, like she's trying to look taller than me.

Nate whispers, "You okay?" right before the three men reach us.

"I'll live."

"Am I allowed to hate your sister?"

I laugh, wishing I could swallow the lump lodged deep in my throat. "The jury's still out. Who are these guys?"

"My bosses. You're looking at Bruce Keaton, Robert Keaton, and Terrence McGill in the flesh."

Why does this cause a spike of nerves? Maybe it's the way the oldest man looks between Jocelyn and me like he can't believe his luck. Maybe it's the way the youngest of the three smirks at Nate's hand on my hip. The third man has a nice smile, though. And Nate introduces him first.

"Mom, Dad, this is my boss, Terrence McGill. And this is Bruce Keaton and his son, Robert Keaton."

"Keaton, Keaton, and McGill," Mr. Cruz says. "We're glad you could make it on such short notice." They all shake hands.

"And this is my date, Juliet Shippe," Nate says, holding me in a way that almost feels proud, "and her sister and new brother-in-law, Jocelyn and Zach Whitley."

Nate says their names quickly, like they're an afterthought, and I definitely shouldn't love it as much as I do.

Bruce drains his champagne glass, sets it on a passing tray, and grabs another before looking at Jocelyn and me again. I press closer to Nate.

Terrence asks Nate's parents about business and travel. He highlights a few of Nate's recent successes, and his parents beam. Nate doesn't think his parents are sincere, but I don't see what he sees. Mr. and Mrs. Cruz look elated to hear anything about Nate, not just his successes. They're as happy hearing Terrence tell them a funny story about Nate as they are hearing how he found a loophole that helped a client avoid litigation. Terrence seems to genuinely appreciate Nate's work, and as Bruce and Robert shift their attention to the conversation, I could almost think I imagined their leering.

Terrence's conversation reaches a natural lull, though, and Bruce again looks between Jocelyn and me.

"You two must get a lot of attention everywhere you go."

Bruce says. "Nate, you didn't tell us you had a girlfriend or that she has a twin." Jocelyn laughs and plays with her necklace while I try not to shudder. She's still standing stick straight. It looks almost uncomfortable.

"I'm not sure there was time for a discussion between the Raymond Industries contracts and the governance docs for Hardison."

Terrence looks over at Robert. "I thought you were doing the Hardison docs?"

"I delegated to an associate." He shrugs, and Terrence frowns.

I feel rather than hear Nate huff. I wonder if Terrence knows how often Robert "delegates" to his associate.

Robert asks Nate's dad something, and Terrence turns to Nate's mom, but Bruce's gaze flits between Jocelyn and me.

"So, my dears, tell me about yourselves," Bruce says. He takes a big drink of his champagne. I wonder how many he's had.

"I'm an accountant with BRG." Jocelyn says.

Bruce's glossy eyes widen. "Beautiful and smart. Well done."

"Thank you," she preens. Zach puts his arm on her shoulder, and, if possible, she looks even stiffer. How is she not throwing up at this man's attention? "I think you know the Whitleys, don't you, Mr. Keaton? Zach will finish law school in May."

So that's why Jocelyn isn't grossed out. She's busy working angles for her husband's future career. She's the perfect wife for men in Zach and Nate's stratosphere. She knows how to draw attention to herself and then shift it to her husband so they can climb that social ladder all the way to the top.

Bruce tells Zach to call him when he passes the bar and then fixes his attention on me. "And you?"

"I'm studying economics at Loyola and interning with *Water Works*. They're a nonprofit that provides access to water in rural and remote areas of Third World countries."

"You're in college?" Bruce smiles into his champagne flute. "You carry yourself with such maturity."

I want to bleach my soul.

"That's because I'm not college-aged," I say. "I'll be twenty-five in March."

"And where did you two meet? Was Nate cruising the campus?" he asks with a condescending laugh.

Jocelyn and Zach laugh with him.

If she'd slapped me, it couldn't hurt worse than her laughing at his joke. I'm glad Nate's parents aren't listening. I wish Nate wasn't, either. If I weren't so flighty, I'd be in a career right now, and this awful old man would get bored with me like he did with Jocelyn. She's too smart to fall for his tactics, but he doesn't think I am. He's fixating on me because he sees me as an easy target.

I'm every bit as young and stupid as he thinks I am.

"Mr. Keaton, that's beneath you," Nate says sharply. "We live in the same building and met in the elevator."

"Love in an elevator." He smiles innocently and finishes his champagne.

But the reference isn't lost on me.

Or Nate.

"That's enough, Bruce," Nate says. "Don't you dare talk to my girlfriend like that."

"*Excuse me?*" he asks. "Don't you dare talk to *me* like that."

"We're done here," Nate says.

"Nate, don't," I whisper urgently. "It's not worth it."

"*You're* worth it. I couldn't care less what this washed up excuse for a man thinks," Nate says. He interrupts Terrence and Robert. "Gentlemen, Bruce has been over-served. It's time for him to leave."

Nate's parents look alarmed, but they don't look as concerned as Terrence. Robert merely looks annoyed.

"What did you do, Dad?" he mutters.

"Nate's dating a college student with a *twin*. He's asking for the attention."

Jocelyn titters, but this time, at least she has the sense to look uncomfortable.

"What did you say?" Mrs. Cruz asks. "What does my son's girlfriend's age have to do with anything?"

I hate this. I hate every second of this. I want that memory-wiping device they have in the *Men in Black* movies so I can permanently erase this conversation from everyone's minds. They may be defending me, but there's no way this won't impact how they see me.

How have I managed to ruin Nate's job and his parents' anniversary party, and all while my sister has a front row seat?

I

Want

To

Cry.

Bruce holds his hands in the air in a defensive position. The lights aren't too dim to hide his red-rimmed eyes.

"Calm down," Bruce says.

"Does my wife not *look* calm?" Mr. Cruz asks. He flags down security, snaps, and points.

"She does, she does," Bruce says. "I meant no offense."

"Then what did you mean?" Mrs. Cruz says, parking herself firmly between Bruce and me.

Security is almost to us when Bruce says, "I was only trying to compliment Nate on his girlfriend. This is all a misunderstanding."

"It's not a problem," I say, wanting this all to end.

But Mrs. Cruz looks at me and grabs my hand, giving it a protective, affectionate squeeze I don't deserve. "That's very big of you. I'm not so forgiving." Security has arrived, but Mrs. Cruz holds a hand up, stopping them so she can address Bruce. "Mr. Keaton, I understand it can feel threatening when a woman doesn't receive a compliment from a man such as yourself, one who thinks he's far more important than he is. Rather than throwing proverbial spaghetti at the wall and seeing what HR or the law lets you get away with, you should stop altogether."

"I'll take that into consideration, Mrs. Cruz," he says in a smarmy tone. "And again, please accept my apologies."

Terrence apologizes profusely, and even Robert gives a quick "Sorry." As security escorts them out, Nate removes his arm from around me.

"One minute," he says.

"Nate—"

But he's already striding for the managing partners at his firm. He weaves between guests until he reaches them, and I watch as he talks, gesturing as big as he did that night in the elevator.

Nate is telling them off, not me.

I am pathetic.

I see Terrence nod before the three men leave, and the pain in my throat from all these unshed tears is taking over my body.

When Nate returns, his face is almost glowing with the fire of justice served.

"What did you say?" Zach, of all people, asks.

"I quit. After I told Terrence exactly what I thought of both Bruce *and* Robert."

Nate stops inches in front of me. "Are you okay?"

"Of course I am," I lie. *I will not cry!* "He's a gross old jerk. Nothing he said means anything. You shouldn't have quit over me."

"You're right," he says, folding me into a hug. "But only because I should have already quit over the fact that I hate contract law."

With my face pressed against his neck, it's almost impossible not to break down. I get the sense that he would do anything for me, and I don't deserve it. I'm as useless as my family thinks, as small as Bruce wanted to make me.

"You okay, sis?" Jocelyn asks. How dare she act concerned after all that?

I smile. "Fine!" The effort to be bright is more tiring than a marathon. I have to force every muscle in my face to do the opposite of what it wants. The strain is giving me a headache. "It was so fun to see you tonight!"

When Joce blinks, I think I see the corner of her lips tug downward. But it must be the light, because nothing about my sister could care how humiliating and hurtful this moment was for me. My failures are her triumphs.

"Okay. We're going to find Zach's parents. See you tomorrow?"

"Sure thing!"

Zach and Jocelyn make their excuses to leave, and even though anyone else would want her sister's support, I'm relieved she's gone.

It's not her fault this happened, but this is yet another mess up she can bear witness to. And boy, will she ever.

Nate's mom and dad huddle around us.

"Juliet, you did nothing wrong," Mrs. Cruz says. "It's kind of you to worry about Nate's job, but you deserve better than that, and any man who would choose a job over you is the wrong man." She looks at her son. "I'm proud of you."

"It was the absolute least I could do. I should have punched him in the throat."

I pull back. "No, you shouldn't have! He'd have sued you!"

"Best money I'd ever spend. He had no right to speak to you like that."

I'm itchy with the need to make this conversation end.

"Men like that think they can say and do whatever they want." Nate's mom says, looking carefully at me. "Now, do you want to come with me to freshen up? I want to sharpen my lashes into daggers after that."

I smile. How does Nate not think his mother is the most amazing woman in the world? "I'm okay, but thank you, Mrs. Cruz."

She holds my gaze just long enough that I know she doesn't miss the tears welling in my eyes. "I like you, Juliet. I hope we'll see you again very soon."

I'm sick as I watch her walk away. Because as much as I've loved meeting her, I'm too humiliated to ever want to see any of these people again.

What has two thumbs and ruins everything?

This girl.

CHAPTER FIFTEEN

NATE

*J*uliet is not okay.

She's hid it well for the last hour, but no matter how many times I've asked her if she wants to take a break or step outside or even go home, she insists everything is fine and that she wants to be here to celebrate with my parents. And whenever we're around lawyers, she hints at how lucky they would be to have me on their staff.

When the Illinois Attorney General tells us how hard she works to retain good state attorneys, Juliet says, "You know, Nate is an incredible attorney."

"Believe me, if I could poach him from KKM, I would in a second."

I laugh, although this isn't the worst idea in the world. I would love to be a state attorney. Talk about pursuing actual justice. "I'll let you know if I'm in the market."

"Please do," she says.

The next time Juliet tries to drop a hint, though, I deflect it and pull her aside afterward.

"Stop feeling guilty and stop trying to find me a new job," I tell her.

"You need a new job, and I'm allowed to feel guilty."

"You're allowed to feel however you feel, even if you're wrong. But you *are* wrong."

She pulls me outside onto the terrace, anger sparking from her like static from a rubbed balloon. It's not snowing, but it is freezing. The patio heaters help, but I still take off my suit jacket and drape it around her shoulders.

"Thank you," she says, hugging her arms around her chest. The city lights illuminate us as much as the lights from the grand ballroom. "And I'm *not* wrong. Nate, you quit tonight because of me! I am the worst fake girlfriend—"

"It's not fake."

"Fine. Worst … *date* ever. My own sister saw what a joke I was!"

"Your sister compounded everything *and* laughed about it. She's the joke."

"Don't say that about her."

"I'll think it, instead."

"Nate, you don't get it, because we haven't known each other that long, but this is what I do. I ruin everything. I touch gold and it turns to brass. My grandma—"

"You saved your grandma. If you hadn't noticed her symptoms when you got back from that walk, who knows what would have happened?"

"My majors—"

"Can't hold your interest because you loved nursing and still miss it."

"My entire childhood—"

"Wasn't what it should have been because your parents didn't understand you."

"Stop interrupting me, and stop trying to make me sound so noble!" she snaps. I bite my tongue in spite of every instinct to the contrary. "I'm a mess, okay? I'm a dumpster fire in the middle of a train wreck. I ruined your parents' party and your career in five minutes just by *existing*. I can't do this, Nate."

"You can't do what?"

"Us! What else will I ruin? I'll probably cost your parents their entire fortune!"

A cold gust blows, and Juliet shivers. I'm too mad to feel the chill, though. I'm boiling over.

"You've been looking for a way out since the moment I told you I was interested."

"Not true."

My hands fly out, speaking a language of their own. "It's absolutely true. All that talk about how you've never had a real boyfriend and how your family teases you about always having a new crush. It's all your way of keeping me at arm's length. But you're not fooling me, Juliet. You're not fooling yourself, either."

"What do you mean?"

"I mean you glow when you see me. You can't keep your eyes off me when I'm in a room. You can't keep your hands off me when I'm near. You've found excuse after excuse to see me since that night on the elevator. You decorated my apartment."

"Because we're friends. Because you're … hot. Because you didn't have Christmas decorations up, and that's a travesty. All of these have explanations."

"You're lying to yourself again, and you know it."

Her frown overtakes her whole face. "You see me as better than I am. You think all of these broken pieces have a reason, but that's because of the world you come from. Everyone has to have a reason for everything they do, because no one is allowed to make a mistake. Maybe I came broken. Have you thought of that? Maybe I'm wrong about everything because I'm an idiot,

135

not because I'm a genius. Maybe I'm just the flighty bozo everyone sees me as."

"You don't need a reason to make a mistake. You're human. We all make mistakes with or without a reason for them."

"Like I did quitting nursing?"

I throw my hands up. "Yes! Everyone thinks you made a mistake quitting nursing! I wasn't there, but it sure seems like you loved it. I don't think being scared to make a mistake is a good reason to stop doing something."

"In healthcare, mistakes can literally kill people."

"You're overstating your role. And you're forgetting all the people you could save."

Her chin quivers. "I loved my nursing rotations. I love helping people. When my grandma had her stroke, it almost ended me, Nate. So yes, maybe I'm so scared to make a mistake that I won't ever fully commit to anything. I'm terrified that if I care about something and mess it up again, I'll never get over it."

"Something?" I take a step closer to her. "Or someone?"

Her eyes water. "You."

I take her cold hands in mine, willing her to stop spiraling.

"I'm scared, Nate. I'm scared that I'm going to find some-thing out about you that changes my mind. What if you pick your nose or don't say 'bless you' when I sneeze or you have nasty garlic breath?"

"I don't pick my nose, I do say 'bless you,' but I absolutely get garlic breath. And I stink after I work out. And I probably snore. I accept that you're human, and you'll have to accept that I am, too. You will never know every fact there is to know about me. You will never be able to predict how I'll react in every possible scenario, and I will never know that about you. But I don't need to know what you'll do if you get a flat on the freeway at three a.m. I only need to know *you*. I only need to know if you want to be with me."

"I can't answer that. There are too many variables."

"There aren't. There's you and me and who we are together. Those are the variables."

"Nate, I mess up *everything*. I can't mess us up, too."

"Juliet, I hate to say this, but we will both mess up constantly. Relationships are a laboratory for love. We'll work on perfecting a formula for years before we get it right just to find out there are a hundred other formulas that need tweaking."

"You're too important to risk a lab explosion. You're too important to risk me missing the signs of you going into a diabetic coma or—"

"So you think the answer to my being *too* important is to break up with me?"

"We're not dating."

"Yes, we are! You know we are. We care about each other. We lo—"

I stop. I can't believe I'm trying to convince her that we love each other and should be together. I can't convince her that she loves me, even if I know she does. I feel it in the marrow of my bones.

But that does nothing if she doesn't want it to. She's provoking a fight. She's looking for a way out, and I cannot let it work.

I can't.

But it's driving me crazy.

"I take it back. You're right. We aren't dating, so you can't break up with me tonight. My parents want me to come over for Christmas Eve tomorrow. I would love for you to come with me, but if you don't want that, I understand."

"My family has Christmas Eve plans. And Christmas."

Her words feel like the first crack of ice on a pond. I don't want either of us falling in.

"I get that. I don't need you to put me above your whole family." Yet. "Let's keep the status quo. *Not* fake dating, *not* not dating, whatever double negative you need to call us. We can keep that going for two days to give us time to take a beat, breathe, and figure this out. Right?"

Juliet looks like she could bolt at any second. I lean back an inch or two to give her space to make this decision.

"Right."

I hold back the violent exhale that begs to release and instead blow it out of my puckered lips like I'm blowing through a straw. "Do you want me to take you home?"

"I'm going to have an Uber come get me."

"Juliet, please—"

The anxiety vibrating off her seems to calm slightly. "I'm okay, Nate. But you're right. You've been the only thing that's existed to me over the last, what, eight days? I feel like I've gone through a year of therapy during that time."

I give her a crooked smile.

"I'm okay," she repeats. "But I think you're right that we should take a couple of days to celebrate Christmas with our families. Let's see what all this *unsanctioned therapy* has done for me."

"All right." It's not the answer I want. Not even close. But it's better than the one I was afraid of. I worry it might be her way of ghosting me. I don't have a choice, though. I love her. I can't let the fear of the end keep me from the journey. "Do you want to wear my jacket home?"

A war rages on her face, and my guts twist waiting for her response.

Wear it, I plead. *Wear it.*

"Thanks. I'll give it back to you after Christmas."

Juliet gives my hands a squeeze and then releases them. No goodbye hug, no kiss on the cheek, no lingering look. She just turns and leaves.

But at least she kept my jacket.

CHAPTER SIXTEEN

JULIET

I slept at my parents' house last night so I wouldn't risk seeing Nate.

It's Christmas Eve morning, and I'm moping in my childhood bedroom like I'm sixteen and found out my sister asked the guy I have a crush on to homecoming.

I can't stop thinking about last night.

Bruce being awful.

Jocelyn and Zach laughing at me.

Nate's parents sweeping to my defense.

Nate quitting his job because of me.

Nate quitting his job *for* me.

Nate's strong, gentle hand on my back as he glided me through the evening.

Nate whispering in my ear, stirring my hair against my cheek.

Nate looking at me like he saw through every pretense.

He is a dream man. I couldn't have made him up if I wanted

to, at least in part because he's *not* perfect. He freezes and holds back. He doesn't stop arguing a point even when he's clearly wrong and I'm clearly right.

He's a real, flawed, imperfect person.

And he's absolutely perfect for me.

He was so proud to introduce me to his parents, as if *he* was the one dating up. He supported me, defended me, gave me his jacket without a second thought. What did I do to deserve him?

Nothing. I couldn't deserve him if I tried.

I mope and pine until the smells of Gran's baking are too tempting to ignore. I'm starving, missing Nate, and tired of looking at the Jonas Brothers poster on the ceiling above my bed. (That's not true. I'm never tired of looking at the Jonas Brothers. Sue me.)

I come downstairs and head toward the kitchen. Mom decorates the house beautifully for all holidays, but especially Christmas. There's a huge tree in the open two-story entry, one in the family room, and another in the living room. Garlands and twinkle lights line every entry and doorway. Stockings hang on the fireplace, poinsettias sit on every end table. The whole house smells of spruce, cinnamon, and cider.

We aren't Whitley or Cruz rich, but we have a big, comfortable home that's always been the gathering spot for our extended family, especially since Gran moved in with us last year. Both of my aunts and uncles and a half dozen of my cousins are in the family room playing games. Two of my cousins are married with kids, and their toddlers wander around the house looking for things to destroy and getting angry when their parents do things like smile or give them candy.

Toddlers are wild.

Jingle Bells plays over the home speakers, and when I hear the chorus, I brace myself for my family's favorite pastime: changing the lyrics to make fun of me.

But before it gets to the chorus, I hear Gran say, "Alexa, next song."

Bless you, Gran.

I walk into the kitchen and find Gran surrounded by ingredients for her old-fashioned molasses cookies, my favorite.

"Need any help?" I ask.

"Why don't you start putting the dry ingredients in the bowl," Gran says.

I'm normally not allowed in the kitchen because I tried to "improve" too many recipes in high school. But Gran isn't afraid of my mistakes. Besides, today I'm not feeling experimental so much as nostalgic.

How can I be nostalgic for someone I met a week and a half ago?

How can I miss him more than I've ever missed anyone?

When I was fourteen, I went to stay with my dad's parents at their place in Indiana for a week. Jocelyn didn't come with me, and I felt homesick for the first time in my life. It gnawed at me, making me feel like I was missing a limb.

This is a million times worse.

I feel like I'm aching for Nate from the inside out. It's not a limb that's missing, but a vital organ. I don't know how much longer I can live without it.

I grab a spoon and scoop flour into a measuring cup.

My mom comes in right in time to see me leveling the flour before dumping it into the bowl.

"Did you scoop that flour with a spoon?" Mom asks.

"Yeah, Nate told me to do it that way if you can't weigh the flour. Is that wrong?"

Are Mom's eyes watering? "No! That's exactly right. I've never seen you be so careful in the kitchen."

"It's not a big deal," I say, carefully adding the second cup.

"Where is Nate today?" Mom asks, sitting at the counter.

"With his parents."

"How was their anniversary party last night?"

I shake my head without meaning to.

"Did something happen?" Gran asks.

And of course, that's the moment that Jocelyn and Zach burst through the front door. "We're home from our honeymoon! And we have gifts!" Joce says.

"They got home yesterday," I mumble. Just in time to crash the party.

Surprisingly, Mom doesn't jump up to greet Jocelyn. "We're in the kitchen, sweetie," she says. She keeps her eyes on me. I measure out the baking soda and put it in the bowl. Jocelyn comes in just as I'm pouring salt into the measuring spoon.

"Uh oh, who let Juliet in the kitchen?" Joce laughs.

"That would be me," Gran says.

"Hello, sweet girl!" Mom says, standing to hug my twin and her husband. Jocelyn's smile looks almost pained when Mom releases her. Did she expect more fanfare? "Sit. Tell me everything."

Joce sits on a barstool with Mom while Zach stands behind her. He puts his hand on her shoulder, and she flinches like he electrocuted her. Then she smiles at us. "It was a small shock. He must have picked up some electricity wearing his wool socks. Why don't you go find my dad! You don't want to hear all my gushing."

Zach nods shrewdly. "I get the point."

She blows him a kiss as he leaves the room. "Jules, did you double check the recipe? I hope this isn't a repeat of 'Salty Night.'"

I used a tablespoon instead of a teaspoon once when I was fifteen. Cousin Chad started singing "Salty Night" instead of "Silent Night," and it caught on.

Good times.

"That was a decade ago," Mom says. "I think it's time to let it go."

"Oh!" my sister says. "Right."

Lori, Lacey, and one of my aunts come into the kitchen, joining Mom and Joce at the counter. They're all looking at Gran as if for signs of stroke. What else could account for her letting me in the kitchen, right? Gran looks at me and rolls her eyes.

I love Gran.

"Chad's wife is the literal worst person I've ever met," Lacey says, falling hard on the barstool.

"I can hear you!" Shannon, Chad's wife of six years, yells. "And it's not my fault you suck at Boggle."

"You suck at everything!" Lacey yells. Her mom flicks her ear.

"Shut it, Lace. Joce, tell us everything!" Lori says. "How was Tahiti?"

Joce grins like a pageant queen. "Ugh, it was indescribable," Joce says. She proceeds to gush without going into specifics. "The suite was *so* gorgeous. The resort was *so* phenomenal. And the weather. Oh my gosh. It was *so* warm but overcast, so it wasn't *too* sunny. I haven't been able to warm up since we got home. I cannot believe how freezing it is here!"

Gran turns on the mixer with a smile, stopping Jocelyn.

The second the mixer stops, Gran adds a negligible dash of ginger.

"And the food was *to die for*," Jocelyn says.

Gran turns the mixer back on.

Joce's mouth snaps closed. Irritation flashes on my sister's face, but she snuggles into her white turtleneck with a dreamy look, and I notice that foundation has rubbed into the top of the sweater, right along her chin.

That's odd. Jocelyn and I have pretty nice skin, so we rarely wear foundation. We cover under eye circles with concealer and dab it on the occasional zit. I narrow my eyes. She's not just wearing foundation, it's caked on. I couldn't tell last night in the

143

dim lights of the grand ballroom, but it's practically movie makeup thick. And her skin looks like it's ... flaking? After a week in a humid climate?

Gran turns the mixer off, and the talking resumes.

"You were saying the food was amazing? What was your favorite meal?" Lacey asks.

"The crab—"

Gran turns the mixer back on. Then she titters. "Whoops!"

Gran winks at me, and I cover my snort.

"Are you okay, Gran?" Jocelyn asks.

Gran turns it off. "Old lady hands. I'm all done. Tell us everything, sweetie," Gran says in a syrupy tone.

Jocelyn sighs. "Guys, the crab on the first night was ... I can't even tell you. I will never forget it. I didn't want to eat anything else after that meal."

Why is she being so weird and vague?

"And don't even get me started on the sealife." She tsks and looks heavenward. "Unbelievable. We got up close and personal with dolphins and sea turtles. And there were schools of jelly-fish! Un. Real."

Gran and I roll the dough into balls and dip them in sugar.

"But that's enough about me. Jules, how are you and Nate? It looks like you two had the *best* time at his parents' party last night."

Mom looks between us. "What do you mean? Did you post pictures from last night, Juliet?"

"No," I say, using Jocelyn's favorite fake smile. "Didn't I tell you? Jocelyn and Zach crashed."

"They what?" Mom asks.

"No, we didn't. We were *invited.*"

"I thought your flight didn't get back until this morning," Lori says. "How did you go to the party?"

My sister shifts. "Mrs. Whitley got an invitation for us and arranged for us to take an earlier flight."

"You left paradise for a party with strangers?" Lacey asks.

"It was my sister's boyfriend's parents' party. They're hardly strangers."

Everyone—and I mean everyone—scoffs at this. Cocked heads, narrowed eyes, raised brows.

"Joce was doing a lot of networking for Zach," I say. "Did you like talking to Bruce?"

"Not as much as he liked talking to *you*." Joce says, looking me over like we're about to have a dance off.

"Yeah, you seemed to *love* that. You certainly laughed enough at my expense."

"It's not my fault everyone was obsessed with the twenty-four year old college co-ed."

"Whoa," Mom says, slicing her hands through the air. "What are you two talking about?"

"Nate's boss was hitting on Juliet," Joce says.

"And you *laughed* about it?" Mom's mouth drops open.

But my sister is too busy looking at me with victory in her eyes to notice that everyone else in the room is at least mildly horrified. When did more of the family come into the kitchen? My dad and Zach aren't here, but everyone else is.

"Oh, Juliet, are you okay?" Gran asks.

"I'm fine," I say, and it's truer than it was last night. Something about it being exposed in daylight makes Bruce's sneering and leering seem less powerful. "He was just a nasty old man."

"Nate's practically an old man." Joce snickers. "Isn't he like thirty-five?"

Jocelyn and I haven't been tight for a few years, but this is different. She's not usually outright cruel. She's usually like a jellyfish, with a small sting here and there that I feel for days after but that no one else notices. Now, though, she's all over the place. Comparing Nate to someone like Bruce is so laughable that whatever concern I may have had over our ages disappears.

"He's thirty-one. Seven years older than me."

145

Gran scoffs. "Seven years isn't an age gap unless you're a teenager. Your grandfather was nine years older than me."

Aunt Judy holds up her hand. "I'm six years older than Carl. Should someone call the cops?"

All of my cousins laugh.

"You're right. Seven years isn't bad," Joce says. "We're all rooting for you, Jules. He's such a good guy. I really hope you two can make it."

Her tone is masterful. This is the Jocelyn I met three years ago, the Jocelyn who appeared when she started dating Zach. The family will see her words as supportive without hearing the mocking, skeptical undertone. I want to respond, want to cut her the way she's cutting me. But what's the point? Everyone will see me as petty and broken. Everyone will think she's being gracious and penitent and I'll be the difficult one, like usual.

I wish Nate were here.

His presence is strengthening. It's like a super serum that allows me to withstand anything. But he's not here, because I messed up last night, like I always do.

I stay silent and put the baking sheet in the oven. I'm ready to go back to my room and let everyone talk about how over-dramatic I am.

Except, when I look up, my cousins are staring at Jocelyn.

"That was rude," Lori says.

"Yeah, Joce, did you mean to sound so ... nasty?" Lacey asks.

"What? You guys are nasty all the time."

"No, we're messing around. We do that with everyone, right Shan?" Lori holds out her hand for a high five. Shannon rolls her eyes but slaps her hand. "You, on the other hand, sounded kind of mean," Lori says.

"No! I'm serious." Jocelyn insists. I can't see her flush through the makeup, but it has to be there. "Nate was so cool at the wedding and again last night. He's one in a million. Jules is so lucky."

"That's funny," Gran says, "because when he texted me this morning, he told me he feels lucky to be dating *her*."

Time slows, and now I want to cry for a different reason. Even without being here, he finds a way to support me. "He texted you again?"

"Again?" Mom asks.

"He and I text every day." Gran takes her phone out of her pocket, removes her glasses for the face recognition, grumbles when it doesn't recognize her face, and then slowly types in her password.

I normally have all the patience in the world for how slow Gran is with technology, but watching her try to find her messages and pick Nate's out is murder. I itch to take the phone from her, but I squeeze my fists and wait. Anxiously.

"Here," she says, finally showing us their text thread.

And it *is* a thread. They message several times a day!

Mom's smile is incredulous. "What do you two talk about?"

"It started with him asking for Juliet's favorite foods so he could surprise her. But we talked about Jeopardy at the wedding, and now we text about it every night. He taught me how to send GIFs."

I laugh as I see *all* of the GIFs Gran has sent. Angry faces. People flipping tables. Babies laughing. People pointing and mocking.

Gran can GIF like a millennial.

But not all of these exchanges are about Jeopardy. There's one about the matchmaking Santa puppy movie that makes laughter explode from me. And the most recent exchange isn't about Jeopardy. It's about me. Gran asked how things went last night, and Nate said he feels like the luckiest guy in the world that I've spent any time with him at all. He hopes he can have a lifet—

Lacey plucks the phone out of my hand.

WHAT DID THAT SAY? Did that say a lifetime?

147

DOES NATE WANT A LIFETIME WITH ME?

I want to lunge for it, but I can't risk alerting everyone to the exchange. Gran snaps her fingers and reaches for the phone before they can get to the end.

"Are you making fun of contestants?" Lacey asks, laughing.

"I am. Nate's too nice for real smack talk."

I hold my hand out, hoping Gran will show me the phone, but she slips it back in her pocket, pretending she didn't see my hand when I know she did.

Sneaky, sneaky Gran.

Lori sighs. "He really is the perfect guy."

"He's not *that* great," Jocelyn says. "He didn't stop his boss from hitting on Juliet."

"He did," I say. "You didn't notice, because when I tried to stop Bruce by talking to Terrence, you swooped in on the conversation and left me high and dry."

"You didn't," Mom says. "Oh, Jocelyn. Why wouldn't you help your sister?"

"Why didn't *she*?" Jocelyn says. "Nothing ever seems to faze her! Anyone can say anything to her, and she just laughs it off!"

"I didn't last night," I say. Why does me laughing things off bother her? "But you're right. I didn't say anything because I was too afraid of messing things up for Nate, and honestly, I felt stupid," I fight to keep a deep frown off my face. "But Nate stopped him. And he quit. You were there, Joce."

Mom covers her mouth with her hands. "He quit KKM for you? They're the most prestigious firm in Chicago, and he quit?" She looks so happy, it brings tears to my eyes.

I think about how upset Nate's parents were last night and how furious Mr. McGill was. There were a lot of powerful people in that room who saw Mr. Keaton get escorted out. "I don't think they will be for much longer."

Mom gives me a watery smile. "I knew I liked him."

I nod.

Last night, Nate quitting upset me. It made me feel like I had ruined everything for him.

Today, it fills me with the same awe and gratitude I see on Mom's face. And I feel a little pride, too. Something about me has inspired real devotion in a man as impressive as Nate Cruz. He chose me over his job. That's not something I should be embarrassed about. That's something I should be shouting from the rooftops.

"He's the best man I've ever known," I say, feeling like Lizzie Bennett defending Mr. Darcy to her dad. But I don't need to defend Nate, because everyone already agrees.

I need to accept that he loves me.

And I love him.

Holy freaking fruitcake.

I love him.

Am I really this dumb?

He's texting my grandmother that he wants a "lifet—" with me, and I'm moping at my house and fighting with my sister?

"What's going on in here?" Dad says as he and Zach come into the room.

Whoa. I didn't notice Zach earlier, because I found him too boring to date and I still find him too boring to pay attention to. But the boy is crab-red.

"Ouch, does that sunburn hurt?" I ask.

Zach stands behind Joce and puts his hands on her shoulders. She winces but tries to cover it. "Let's keep our hands to ourselves, kay sweetheart? I don't want anyone to feel jealous."

"Sure, angel," he says.

Ew.

Does she really call him "sweetheart?" And he really calls her "angel?"

Listen, I can get behind a good nickname. Something clever, like, I don't know, a woman calling her husband "Pinky" because he secretly loves her pink bra, or something. But in the absence of an established inside joke, "babe" is the *only* acceptable pet name.

"And yes," Zach says. "The sunburn hurts like a beast, but it's nothing compared to Joce's. She looks like she has boils. She picked the wrong trip for a string bikini."

Gran has a coughing fit, and I turn around to pat her back so we can both cover our laughter.

"It's not that bad," Jocelyn says. This explains her makeup. "Who knew that you can get so burned on overcast days?"

"Um, everyone," Lacey says with a laugh. "How was the food? Jocelyn told us about the crab."

"She did?" Zach asks. "I thought we weren't mentioning the food poisoning."

"Food poisoning?" Lori asks. "Joce said the food was to die for."

"Yeah, literally. We got salmonella. That's why we cut the trip short. We almost had to go to the hospital for IV fluids. That stuff was coming out both ends. We barely got to see the resort."

"But you guys liked the sealife, right?"

"We got attacked by a school of jellyfish on day one. It was the worst trip of my entire life. Tahiti can go suck an egg."

"It wasn't that bad!" Joce protests. But I can't see her face, because Gran and I are doubled over, laughing so hard, neither of us can breathe. "The resort was gorgeous!"

"The bathroom wasn't when we finished with it."

Gran drops behind the island, howling with laughter. I collapse in a fit next to her, tears streaming down my face.

"And then you made us go to that stupid party last night and kept trying to convince all of those firms to hire me? You made me look like an idiot!"

"I was *networking*."

"You were hitting them over the head with a hammer, except the hammer was *me*."

"Well, maybe if you spent less time playing *Madden* and more time studying, I wouldn't have to *hammer* anything."

"Oh, this again? Come on, Joce."

"Guys," Dad says over their arguing. "Why don't you two take your fight somewhere else."

"We're not fighting!" Jocelyn snaps.

"Okay, sweetie," Dad says. I can't see the smile on his face, but I can hear the heck out of it. "Juliet, Gran, are you two still with us?"

"No," Gran says. "I've fallen and I can't get up."

My parents, aunts, and uncles all laugh at this.

I help Gran up, and we wipe tears of laughter from our faces.

My twin looks like she wants to set fire to the house. I look closer.

Wait, that's not anger. That's humiliation.

Seeing such pain on her face is like feeling it in my heart.

Jocelyn is hurting.

This isn't just a disappointing week. This is bigger than that. I step around the counter and in front of my sister. Suddenly, I don't want to take joy in her pain.

Her pain is my pain.

"I'm sorry, Joce. Your honeymoon should have been the best week of your life, and it sounds like it was a nightmare. Salmonella is really serious. How are you feeling?"

Joce's huge green eyes well with tears and a sob escapes her throat. "Horrible. I'm so tired, Jules. I had two Monsters last night to try to perk up, but then I couldn't sleep, and now I feel like my heart is going to explode."

"We shouldn't have gone to the party," Zach says, his voice softer.

"Your mom threatened to cut us off if we didn't!"

"She threatens to cut me off twice a month, but she'd never do it. She cares too much about what people think. Why else do you think she made us go to the party last night? She didn't want Nate's girlfriend to steal the show." He nods at me.

Mom raises her eyebrows, and Zach shrugs.

"Yeah, my mom's a puppet master. I can't stand it. I only went last night because I thought you wanted to see Juliet."

Jocelyn looks at her feet before looking up at me. She swallows heavily. "I'm sorry, Jules. I've been a terrible sister. I don't think you're a mess, I think you're lost. I should have helped you find your way, but instead, I think I've made it all worse."

The lump in my throat swells, and emotion pricks the back of my eyes. "Let's talk about this in the bathroom while I help you with this burn, okay?"

She nods, crying. "Okay."

I drag her into the bathroom and lift her sweater up. And gasp.

Her entire back is covered in big, thick blisters. How is she not weeping from pain?

"Don't pop any of the blisters or they could get infected. And why on earth are you wearing a wool sweater?"

"Because it's Christmassy."

"Christmassy? Joce, this is the itchiest substance you could put on, and you have an extremely sensitive burn." I rifle through the cabinet beneath the sink and pull out the aloe vera. I help her remove her sweater and start slathering it on her back around her bra. I text Mom to send in the softest, most over-sized cotton sweatshirt she can find. "Why did wearing something festive matter so much?"

My sister looks at me in the mirror, and even though I can spot the few differences between us, we blur together, like when you look at a 3D image and something new emerges.

"I know it must suck having people tease you about being difficult, but it's not easy having everyone expect me to look and act a certain way all the time. I'm the 'easy one!' The easy one always does what everyone wants her to do. I can't make waves. I can't ever protest. I have to smile when they want me to smile and wear what they expect me to wear."

"I didn't know."

"Meeting everyone's expectations is the only thing I know how to do. Like accounting. I never wanted to get a master's in it. I never intended for it to become my career. But everyone was so excited that I had an A in such a hard class, and Zach's parents were so impressed that he was 'finally dating someone smart,'" she says in air quotes. "So I declared accounting as my major to impress them. That was right around the time you quit nursing and everyone acted like you'd had a nervous break- down, and the last thing I wanted was for them to look at me like that."

I sniff. "Yeah, I get that."

"Jules, why didn't you say how much you were hurting? You laughed with us instead of telling us to stop. You were too nice."

"Why did you stop being on my side? It was always us against them!"

She bites the inside of her cheek. "I didn't want Zach to see me like that. And honestly, it hurts when they make fun of me. I don't get how you have such a thick skin about it."

"I don't! It hurts me, too, but I realized how you all saw me and I was trying to be the easy one."

Joce frowns, tears spilling down her face. "And we wouldn't let you." She sobs. "I'm sorry. If you'd pushed back, we all would have stopped."

"Would you have? Honestly?"

She wipes her face with a tissue. Her makeup comes with it. "I don't know. But I hope we would have."

"You all blamed me for Gran's stroke."

"What?" Joce turns around, horror written all over her face. "No, we didn't!"

"Yes, you did! I heard you all talking about it in the hospital waiting room."

She shakes her head adamantly. "No, I swear. No one blamed you. Weren't you walking Chad's disgusting dog?"

"She'd already had the stroke when I left." The tightness I know too well squeezes my lungs. "And in the hospital, I heard you ask what the point of nursing school is if someone misses something so obvious!"

Joce looks away, like she's racking her brain. Then she gasps. "That was the nurse in the ER! She asked if Gran had any other conditions and we showed her the medic alert bracelet that said she's deathly allergic to penicillin. We were talking about *her*."

Shock roots me in place, numbing me from the tips of my toes up to the top of my head. "You guys weren't talking about me? You didn't blame me?"

Joce bursts into tears, and I can't help but do the same. "Were we really that awful that you thought we'd blame you?" Joce asks.

Were they?

My family teased me, but if I weren't so scared of making mistakes, if I weren't such a perfectionist, would I have internalized my fear so deeply? I've always been passionate about medicine and helping people, but was I afraid, even then? Did I sabotage myself then just like I'm sabotaging myself with Nate now?

"I don't know."

"But you're not sure? Jules!" she weeps, and that makes me weep.

Maybe we do have a twin bond.

"It's okay," I say. "It'll be okay. As long as it stops. I can't be the family punching bag anymore."

"I promise. Never again."

Mom knocks on the door. "Can I come in?" she asks.

I let Mom slip in and close the door after her. "Oh, sweeties!" she says when she sees us. And then she bursts into tears.

She hugs me so tight, I feel like my broken pieces are being put back together again. She takes Jocelyn's hand, careful not to even graze her burn.

"What were you thinking that you didn't put on sunscreen?"

"I messed up, okay? I'm not perfect!" Joce says.

"I know. And I'm proud of you for it." Mom smiles. Then to me, she says, "But you're so close."

I laugh through my tears.

"I'm so sorry, girls. I didn't know I was putting you in boxes all these years. I didn't see you as the wonderful, complex women you both are. Can you forgive me?"

Joce and I look at each other and nod.

I carry wounds from my family that have stayed open for a long time. When my mom hugged me at Jocelyn's wedding, it was the first time I've felt like someone had put balm over one of those wounds.

Today, I feel like an infection has been cleared from the remaining cuts. They're finally being given the chance to heal.

It feels good.

Mom helps Joce put on an oversized sweater. "We're glad you're home, Jocey." She smiles at my sister. "Now, Juliet, where is Nate? Why haven't you invited him over?"

"Because I'm dumb."

"You are not." Mom pulls me into a hug and talks in my ear a bit too loudly. "You are smart and fabulous, and I won't let *anyone* talk about you that way ever again."

"Thanks, Mom."

The bathroom isn't roomy with the three of us crammed together in front of the vanity, especially with two of us trying to hug without jostling the third's sunburn. We laugh and leave the bathroom together, and for the first time in a long time, I feel good about myself being around my family.

I finally feel like *me*.

CHAPTER SEVENTEEN

NATE

*E*very year on Christmas Eve, my parents volunteer at a charity boxing up food and presents for families. I haven't joined them since I was in law school, but I do today.

I always thought their volunteering was for show, but today, I notice something I didn't pick up on when I last did it with them: there are no cameras.

No one is filming this. This isn't being posted anywhere. My parents are simply here, volunteering their time (and a substantial amount of money) to serve people in need.

"How is Juliet after last night?" Mom asks. Hairnets aren't attractive on anyone, but she's as confident wearing it as she is wearing a diamond tiara (she owns three).

"We didn't end the night in the best place," I say, placing containers and cans of food into a large box.

"Why not?"

Mom probes a lot into my life, and I typically don't have much to tell her. Work. Bland dates. Repeat. On a whim, I told her about Mrs. Kikuchi several months ago, and it was the most we've talked in years. She had a hundred questions about "the dear woman who looks out" for me. She even sent her a birthday present.

I'm not sure why she cared to hear about Mrs. K, but I know why she cares to hear about Juliet. Mom was there last night, and she defended Juliet. And my dad was beside her, backing up every word. No matter what scars I have from my childhood, my parents scored big points in my book last night.

"She has all the classic signs of being gifted, including being an utter perfectionist. She thinks she ruined my career and now she worries she's going to ruin things with us, too."

"Poor thing. That's a lot to navigate. It reminds me a little of someone else I know."

"Who? Dad?"

"No, you."

I stock another box.

"Me? I'm not a perfectionist."

"No, but you have your quirks, too. You're so obsessed with achievement that you never take a break to evaluate what you need."

"I'm not like that."

"You are, *filhinho*," she says. *Little son.*

Dad comes over to work next to us. "You're exactly like that, son. When you were little, you were always so worried about getting in trouble at our parties, and you made us tell you over and over again what you could say or do that would make the evening go as well as possible. We figured we must have talked too much about events and unknowingly put those anxieties on you. But even after we stopped talking about them, you held on to that fear. 'What can I do to make sure the night goes perfectly, Papá? Who should I talk to? What do you want me to say?' It was so much pressure! So we told you that the only thing

157

you had to do was sit in the corner and read, and everything would be perfect."

"Except, you took that to an extreme and thought it meant the night could *only* be perfect if you sat in the corner and read." Mom rolls her eyes affectionately. "You always took things too far."

I think back to all the times I sat in the corner of a party, my spine stick straight, my nose stuck in a book. All those times that my parents came over and told me how well I did, how I made such a difference at the event … they were trying to put my mind at ease? They were trying to spare me the anxiety of performing for a crowd before I was ready or willing?

All these years, I thought they *demanded* strict obedience from me.

In reality, they were trying to help *me* not demand such strict obedience from *myself*.

"You're right," I whisper. "You're absolutely right."

"What did you think we were doing all this time?" Mom asks.

"I thought I was a prop you pulled out for photo opportunities and put back on a shelf."

Mom's eyes and mouth widen and widen some more, and then she bursts into tears. *"Meu amor!"* She zips around the boxes between us and throws her arms around me. "I am so sorry! I should have talked to you! I should have told you! I thought you preferred to sit back. I didn't know! Oh, *meu filho!"*

I give her a watery laugh, but hug her tightly. "I should have told you how I felt."

Dad joins in on the hug. "No, you shouldn't have. We're your parents. It was our job to see you, and we didn't. Don't you dare blame yourself for our failings."

The tears in my eyes don't fall. My smile is too big to give them room. My mom kisses my cheeks and tells me over and over how much she loves me. My dad squeezes me tightly and says how I've always been a credit to the family.

"You are the only thing that matters," Dad says. "I'd give every penny away for your happiness."

"I'd keep a few of the pennies," Mom teases. "No, I'd give everything away for you." She puts her hands on my cheeks and looks up at me, our brown eyes a mirror of one another's. "We love you."

"*Chega*," I say with a laugh. "*Basta*. Enough. We have more boxes to pack."

"It's not all about work, *mi hijo*," Dad says. "You worked for KKM for seven years, and you gave them your all, but I'm proud of you for quitting. You're finally looking at what *you* want and need."

"I need a job."

"No, you *want* a job," Mom corrects me. "You never need to work a day in your life, although we hope you'll find something fulfilling to do eventually."

"Like maybe being the head of legal for our nonprofit," Dad says, and for the first time in years, his suggestion doesn't feel controlling or manipulative. It feels like he simply misses me.

I miss them, too.

I smile. "It's not the worst idea."

"Think it over, but there's no pressure," Dad says.

"And in the meantime," Mom says, "you should go visit Juliet."

"You guys really liked her?"

"Liked her?" Mom stops her work. "We loved her! She's funny and smart and makes you happy. What isn't there to like?"

"The better question," Dad says, "is do *you* really like her."

"I love her. It's barely been a week, but I knew that first night on the elevator."

"How did you know?" Dad asks. "A single night on an

elevator could lead easily to fascination, but why do you think it's love?"

This question has run through my mind a lot in the hours and days since I met Juliet. I always thought she was attractive when I saw her around the building, but I was too annoyed to appreciate anything good about her. Starting from a place of only seeing her flaws has helped me see how her strengths add to her and flesh her out as a well-rounded, complex, vexing, amazing woman.

She'll do anything for the people she loves. To a fault, she'll sacrifice her pride for someone else's happiness or comfort. She'll blame herself before pointing a finger at others.

But she'll also argue a point she doesn't believe for the sake of understanding you.

She'll do the floss in your face when she beats you at Skip-Bo.

What's not to love?

"I see her. And she sees me."

Dad smiles, grabbing the last box. "Then go tell her."

"And bring her home, *meu amor*," Mom adds.

We finish packing the final box together, and then I hug my parents.

And run.

* * *

I think about texting Gran for the address to the Shippe's home, but I go back to my apartment to shower, first.

After four hours of manual labor, I stink.

Also, I bought a present that I can't wait to give Juliet.

Also …

I forgot that we agreed to talk after Christmas, not after twelve hours.

I finish my shower slowly and get ready even slower. There's no point in rushing. Juliet isn't going to see me today. I step out to the fire escape and breathe deeply, getting a lungful of exhaust with hints of crisp, earthy snow. It snowed all last night and is expected to continue through tomorrow. The world has that intense brightness that you can only see on a snowy day.

My phone buzzes, and it's a text from Gran.

It's a GIF of the Sicilian from *The Princess Bride* saying "Inconceivable."

Huh?

A moment later, there's another text.

GRAN: Whoops!! Old lady hands!!

GRAN: *GIF of a meteor headed for earth*

What is she talking about?

GRAN: *GIF of a sideline reporter getting pegged with a football*

GRAN: *GIF of a cat falling on a man's head with the words "brace for impact"*

Did one of her great grandkids take her phone? No, she said "old lady hands," which means this is her.

NATE: I think I'm too old to understand. What's going on?

. . .

GRAN: INCOMING!!!!!!!!

GRAN: Juliet's on her way!!!!!!

Excessive use of exclamation points. That's Gran.

Juliet's on her way here?

Shoot! I left her present in the car!

I run out of my apartment and head straight for the stairs, out to the parking garage, and into my car. I grab the present and run back in. I'm halfway up the stairs—my thighs and lungs on fire—when I realize I left my keys in my car.

I slap my palm to my face, holding the railing and panting for a minute.

No, it's okay. Mrs. Kikuchi has my spare key. Her son and his family are coming over today, but she won't mind if I stop by for ten seconds to get my key. I text her as I continue up the stairs. She replies with a thumbs up.

On the twelfth floor, her two grandkids are racing up and down the hallway. Mrs. Kikuchi and her son and daughter-in-law are all talking outside her apartment door. I smile at them and try to catch my breath. I thought I was so in shape, but I've learned in the last week that gym muscles are not the same thing as fifteen-flights-of-stairs-multiple-times-a-day muscles.

"You took the stairs?" her son, Ken, asks. We've met several times, and he shakes my hand.

"Long story." I breathe in deeply. "Sorry to interrupt. I can't believe I forgot my keys in the car."

Mrs. K looks at me knowingly. "I bet I can guess what you're thinking about. Or who."

"Right, as always. Thanks for letting me barge in."

"It's okay," she says. "I'm glad we had a chance to see each other before ... before I move at the end of the month."

My stomach drops faster than a roller coaster. "You're moving? What happened? I thought we worked everything out with the landlord."

"You did," Ken says. He gestures to his wife. "We recently bought a bigger place and it has plenty of room for Mom. We all miss her too much not to have her around."

"And I'm a good babysitter," Mrs. K adds with a wink. Then her smile falls. "I'll miss you, Nate. Will you and Juliet visit?"

"I will," I promise, giving this wonderful surrogate mother a big, tight hug. "I'll do my best to have her with me."

"She'll be there," Mrs. K says, her voice thick. "You two are meant to be."

"Love you, Momma K."

"Love you, too, dear boy."

I leave them with a few more hugs and waves and head straight to the elevator, my mind dwelling on the bittersweet knowledge that this dear woman will be with her family but not with me.

The elevator doors open, and my feet lead me on. I'm about to press the button when I notice another pair of feet.

Actually, they're slipper boots.

I follow the slippered feet up to a pair of Christmas pajamas, a pair of bright green eyes, and gorgeous blonde hair stuffed under a beanie.

"What are you doing here?" Juliet asks. Her incredulous smile pulls wider and wider.

"I live here."

"No, I mean on the elevator!"

"I was distracted."

She laughs. "Oh, were you?"

"Mrs. K is moving in with her son and his family."

Her smile falters. "I thought you meant—never mind. That makes sense."

"Jules. Of course I was also distracted thinking of you. But I haven't stopped being distracted by thoughts of you since the last time I got on this metal death box."

Relief smoothes the lines on her forehead. "I missed you."

I take one of her hands in mine, holding her gift behind my back with the other.

"I missed you, too."

Juliet holds my gaze. "I don't want fake with you, Nate. I want us to be real, all the way. But I don't know how to do this. I'm scared of messing up and pushing you away."

"You won't push me away."

"How do you know?"

"Because you love me, and I love you."

She seems to glow from within. "I *do* love you."

"I knew it!"

She laughs. "Wow, gloating much?"

"Says the girl who did the entire suite of Fortnight dances after beating your cousins at Old Maid?"

"Exactly. I know it when I see it."

She's teasing, but I'm not. "I do, too."

Her smile tells me she gets what I'm doing. "So, is this real? Are we officially boyfriend and girlfriend?"

"I don't think I want that anymore," I say. Her mouth forms a perfect o. "Juliet, you are an intelligent, gifted, scared perfectionist. You're afraid to see something through, because you're afraid of the mess. What if you can't make every part of it perfect? What if we fight? If you commit, if you really commit, you can't just drop me like a major, and that terrifies you. Am I right?"

"What about you? You chose a career that you only tolerate because you wanted to prove yourself and thought using your family's money would make you less of a man. You're afraid that if you ever did something for yourself, you might have to admit that your parents aren't the monsters you thought they were and you could do a lot more with their money than your pride will allow you to. Sound about right?"

"I'm not arguing."

"*You* aren't arguing?" she asks.

"Hey, come on. We don't fight about everything."

"Just almost everything?"

"Exactly. And Juliet Shippe, I want to fight with you for the rest of my life."

The o on her lips capitalizes. "What do you mean?"

"I love you and I don't want to let you go. Marry me."

"What? Nate. That's crazy!"

"Is it really, though? Can you honestly tell me that saying goodbye instead of goodnight hasn't driven you mad?"

"Absolutely bonkers," she says, running a finger over her bottom lip in the most distracting possible way. "But, I haven't even kissed you yet."

"Yet?"

Juliet throws herself at me. Literally.

CHAPTER EIGHTEEN

JULIET

*M*y lips crash into Nate's and then the heat of our mouths melts us together. He tastes like peppermint and cocoa, and if that's not the makings of a Merry Christmas, I don't know what is. Nate slides his hands around my back while I thrust mine in his hair.

Nate's hair.

Oh my gosh, it is luxurious. It's so thick and soft, I want to bury my face into it, except my face is currently better occupied by Nate's face, and so I content myself with letting my hands have free rein.

And we kiss.

Except, this isn't any kiss. It's not merely greedy lips and hot breath. It's delicious banter that makes me want to squeal and laugh at the same time. It's an enlivening debate that keeps me on my toes and has me guessing and anticipating what he'll do next. It's cuddling under a warm blanket, not just for safety or warmth, but for connection, a stronger connection than I've ever had. It's a conversation where I feel totally seen and completely accepted.

It's an embrace, body and soul.

It's love.

Pure, simple, messy love.

It's perfect.

I don't want to tell him yet, because I'm enjoying the gentle tug of his lips on mine and the way his hands clutch me into him. But as our kisses slow and deepen, I need him to know what this means to me. This is more than a confirmation of what I've known since that night on the elevator. This is a commitment to every promise he wants to make me and every promise he's asking me to make him.

I pull back a fraction of an inch. "Yes."

I go back in for another kiss, but he stops me. "What did you say?"

I feel drunk on his mouth, and his eyelids are heavy enough that I suspect he feels the same. "I said yes. Because I love you, too. I've loved you since you gave me that silly gifted test on the elevator."

"You mean extremely scientific test," he argues.

I scrunch my nose, wanting to bite his lip. "You didn't judge me. You saw me, and you helped me see myself. I've had my head in the clouds for years, but every minute we've spent together, I've fallen harder. You've brought me back down to earth. You've helped me realize who I am and who I want to be. I want you, Nate. I love you. I'm not going anywhere."

Nate's smile stops abruptly. He looks around at the elevator

…

How are we still on the elevator?

"Juliet," he says in a panic. "*We're* not going anywhere. I think we're stuck."

I look at the panel and the floor indicator and laugh. I press the number fifteen and the elevator car starts moving. "We didn't press the button," I say. "I guess we didn't know where we were going yet."

Nate's gaze fuses my soul to his. "We do now."

EPILOGUE

Christmas Day
Nate

*J*uliet's family, my parents, and Mrs. Kikuchi and her family are all gathered around the giant Christmas tree in the grand ballroom of the Windsor Hotel.

Mom and Dad invited everyone to stay the night in the hotel yesterday afternoon, and when the Shippes and Kikuchis realized there's an indoor lazy river and no one would have to do any more cooking or cleaning, everyone agreed.

I spent every Christmas in Chicago in this hotel, sometimes with the hotel staff and their families, other times with family friends who were also staying in Chicago over the holidays.

No matter how many people were in here, it always felt too cavernous and empty.

It doesn't anymore.

The décor is as fancy as ever, but my parents pulled out all the stops, with game tables, a movie screen and popcorn machine, bounce houses for the little kids, and more. The kids were impatient to run around and play until they saw the dozens of extra presents my mom managed to arrange last night. (Don't worry: she gave everyone at each of the stores a five-figure Christmas bonus for their troubles. No one seemed to mind.)

Everyone is sipping hot cocoa in their Christmas pajamas, talking, and waiting to open presents. Juliet's family doesn't quite seem to know how to talk to her, now that they don't dare make her the punch line of every joke. Fortunately, for all of their missteps, they have a lot of love for each other, and it seems like Juliet can finally feel it.

Meanwhile, our parents and Gran and Mrs. K keep giving each other knowing looks, like they can't wait for the moment I get down on one knee.

For the record, everyone knows I already proposed.

I made the mistake of sending Gran a "she said yes" GIF.

When her family burst into the ballroom yesterday evening for the dinner my parents arranged, they all screamed, "You're engaged!"

Gran really is a gossip hound.

The moment she came in, Jocelyn squealed in excitement and hugged Juliet (and then abruptly stopped hugging, because evidently her sunburn is that bad). It made Gran and me a bit misty-eyed.

Most everyone spent the evening on the lazy river and then we all came upstairs to the grand ballroom to watch Christmas movies and stuff our faces before bed. (Mom had a lot of diabetic-friendly treats, as always.)

And now, after a night dreaming of making Juliet mine forever, we're gathered around the Christmas tree.

I look to my parents and Juliet's, but they all gesture back to me.

"Thank you for coming, everyone," I say, sitting on the ground next to Juliet, "especially at the last minute."

"Anytime you want to put us up in suites in the ritziest hotel in Chicago, we're there," Juliet's cousin, Chad, says. His toddler is playing his head like a bongo, and Chad doesn't seem to notice.

I smile. "I know everyone is eager to open presents, but I hope you guys don't mind me giving Juliet hers, first."

"He's going to propose!" Lacey whispers.

"He already did!" Juliet stage-whispers back.

"Oh yeah!"

"What he did not do," Juliet says archly, "is give me a ring."

"I proposed on Christmas Eve after something like nine days. Cut a guy some slack," I say to laughs.

"Hey, I'm like Michael Scott." Juliet says. "I want to be feared *and* loved. I want you to be afraid of how much you love me." And to prove her point, she kisses me, sucking my lower lip into her mouth. And then biting it a little.

Fear and love.

"Mission accomplished," I say. The moment she lets me go, I want to kiss the smug smile off her face.

"Okay, give me the present already."

"It's not that big of a deal," I say. I only commissioned it right after we went shopping together for an obscene amount of money.

"If it's from you, I'm going to love it," she says. "Now gimme."

"Just be careful," I tell her. "It's fragile."

I grab a massive, ornately wrapped present (I have a black belt in gift wrapping) and give it to her. She tears the wrapping off and gets to the box, which she opens more carefully.

There's another wrapped box.

And another.

And another.

Yes, I did the whole nested gift thing. No, I have no regrets.

Watching her nose scrunch in that adorably irritated way she has is more than worth it.

When she finally opens the last box, she pulls out a gorgeous, carefully crafted music box. It's an exact replica of the elevator in our building. The elevator doors are open, and inside it are two faceless figures huddled together (I'm not ashamed that I still love the faceless art trend). Otherwise, they look like Juliet and me, down to the cat sweatshirt and the blankets on our laps.

"How did you do this?" she whispers.

"Money."

Everyone laughs.

Juliet inspects it more closely and pulls a little drawer out from underneath the elevator.

Inside is a ring.

It's bigger than Jocelyn's.

(Sorry Zach.)

I take the ring out of the drawer and she gapes and holds her hand out.

"Yes," she says.

"You said that yesterday."

"Just making sure you got the message the first time."

I slide the ring onto her finger and she kisses me like we're alone.

Very alone.

"A-hem," her mom says.

"Right, sorry about that," I say. "But Jules, you need to listen to the song."

"Is it the one we danced to at Joce's wedding?" she asks, hearts for eyes.

"Uh—"

Shoot. That would have been a much classier idea than the one I picked.

She winds it, and I try to stop her. "What are you doing?"

She laughs, winding it the rest of the way and then biting her lip as she lets go.

The theme from *The Office* plays.

She stares at me, unblinking. "Seriously? We just got engaged, and your first gift to me is an expensive gag gift?"

"Yes?"

She throws back her head, laughing. "I love you more every second, Nate Cruz. Now open my gift."

Her gift to me is in a gift bag. Much more practical. I pull out the tissue papers to find ... papers?

It's a printout of a registration form. "What is this?" I ask.

"Look closely."

I look at the top of the form, and it says it's the Illinois NCLEX-RN exam.

It's the RN exam.

My eyes shoot to hers. "Seriously?"

"I registered to take the exam last night. I have four months to remember everything I forgot about nursing. Think you could help me study now that you have a little time on your hands?"

"It would be my pleasure. My *pleasure* pleasure." I'm about to lean in and kiss her again when Jocelyn groans.

"Okay, enough. We're the freaking newlyweds here, people. Let's move on."

Juliet kisses me anyway, and all around us, people start tearing into their gifts.

We kiss until her cousins heckle us into stopping. I will never want to stop kissing Juliet, but I can handle it for now.

What started as a moment has become the beginning of forever.

THE END

Want more sweet and swoony romcoms? Sign up for my newsletter and get a FREE novella: www.katewatsonbooks.net/newsletter

Let's Connect!
Instagram @KateWatsonBooks
Facebook Clean Romcom Reader Group

And if you enjoyed this book, I hope you'll consider reviewing it on Amazon. Reviews mean the world to indie authors.

ACKNOWLEDGMENTS

I did not plan to write a Christmas book, but Raneé S. Clark and Kaylee Baldwin are the best people to room with at a writer's conference, because, while you will not work as much as you "should," you will come out of it with PLANS. And I love you both for it (and for reading and providing feedback and a million other reasons!).

Sam Ann and Britney M. Mills, thank you for your feedback and discerning eye! And Jen Atkinson and Becky Wallace, thanks so much for help with the blurb when I panicked. You're all wonderful! Sarah Carner, thank you for making writing more manageable! I'm so glad to have found you.

To the amazing bookstagram community—including Meredith, Jenn, Madelyn, Lindsey, Sarah, and Susan—thank you for all the support and boosting. And a huge thank you to my ARC readers! You cannot know what a difference you have made to my career.

My long-suffering husband has put up with a lot in our years together (*cough* England *cough*), and that isn't about to change now that I'm writing even more books. I love you, Jota.

My delightful children, you may not be as long-suffering as your dad, but I love you just as deeply.

As always, I owe everything to my gracious God.

ABOUT THE AUTHOR

Kate Watson is a fan of cheeky romantic comedies and delightfully witty banter. Originally from Canada, she attended college in the States and holds a BA in Philosophy from Brigham Young University. A lover of travel, speaking in accents, and experiencing new cultures, she has also lived in Israel, Brazil, the American South, and she now calls Arizona home.

She started writing at six years old and sold her first book, "The Heart People," for $0.25 to her parents. It received rave reviews. Since then, she's written many books, including the acclaimed Off Script, a 2020 Junior Library Guild selection. She writes stories full of heart, humor, and happily-ever-afters.

She is currently living her own happily-ever-after with her super cute husband and their four wild and wonderful kids. She runs on caffeine, swoons, and Jesus.

ALSO BY KATE WATSON

Sweet as Sugar Maple Series:
Strawberry Fields for Never
Baby Llama Drama

Made in the USA
Middletown, DE
18 December 2023